"TO DIE GAME"
Gen. James Ewell Brown "Jeb" Stuart, CSA

by
Patrick Brennan

Published 1998
Farnsworth House Military Impressions
415 Baltimore Street
Gettysburg, PA 17325
(717) 334-8838

Cover Photo: Valentine Museum, Richmond, VA

Rear Cover: Don Pierce

All photographs cited to their specific repository or donor.

ISBN: 0-891459-02-3

DEDICATION

To

Sheila Brennan

And to the memory
of Sam Sweeney and the musicians
who sang, played, and rode with Jeb Stuart

In his heavenly bivouac, the Camp Qui Vive band
is playing still.

INTRODUCTION

"...Stuart of Laurel Hill,
'Beauty' Stuart, the genius of cavalry,
Reckless, merry, religious, theatrical,
Lover of gesture, lover of panache,
With all the actor's grace and the quick, light charm
That makes women adore him—a wild cavalier
Who worships as sober a God as Stonewall Jackson,
A Rupert who seldom drinks, very often prays,
Loves his children, singing, fighting, spurs, and his wife.
Sweeney his banjo-player follows him."

—Stephen Vincent Benet
John Brown's Body

As the millenium approaches, one can count five Civil War soldiers whose names and exploits have become more or less embedded in the American popular consciousness; to wit: Robert E. Lee, Ulysses S. Grant, Thomas J. "Stonewall" Jackson, William Tecumseh Sherman, and James Ewell Brown "Jeb" Stuart. Looking ahead, it is interesting to speculate which of the mythic five will prove most durable in the coming century. On the strength and accuracy of Stephen Vincent Benet's imagery— quoted above—I suspect that Jeb Stuart may be riding a raid in the national imagination long after memories of the others have grown dim.

Stuart's strong suit is, of course, his never fading youth...combined with his inexhaustable espirit and perpetual drive, qualities which Americans in particular have always admired. Cut down in the prime of his early thirties, Jeb was a man who had lived life to the hilt, with flair and emphasis, never looking back, always willing to confront whatever lay ahead...even the worst. As Stephen Vincent Benet suggests, Stuart's playful, sporting side was ballasted by strong principles, serious religion and a happy, loving marriage. He would "rather die than be whipped," he said, and though he and the Confederacy would perish in the end, he stayed the course and was never whipped in spirit. His life is the stuff of American legend, a legend sure to endure for another century at least.

With this booklet we close the Army of Northern Virginia phase of the Farnsworth House Commander Series. Although there are other commanders to come, with this pamphlet we conclude Confederate campaigning in the east under "Marse Robert". In rounding it off, I would like to extend my thanks to our Army of Northern Virginia authors: Wayne E. Motts (Lewis A. Armistead), Richard F. Selcer (George E. Pickett), Gary W. Gallagher (Robert E. Lee), Robert K. Krick (Thomas J. Jackson), and Carol Reardon (James Longstreet). After four years of ANV editorial campaigning...I bid them and their army an affectionate farewell.

Stuart author Pat Brennan joins me in thanking Robert E. Lee Krick, mapmaker Jim Coudal and all others who assisted in bringing Jeb to life. Our special thanks to Jeb Stuart IV for graciously consenting to provide family perspective along with reflections on his ancestor's role in the shaping of Civil War cavalry.

John S. Peterson, Editor
Farnsworth House Commander Series

VIRGINIA, YOUTH—WEST POINT

On February 6, 1833, James Ewell Brown Stuart was born at Laurel Hill, a farm in rural Patrick County, Virginia. The seventh of eleven children, he was surrounded by the strength of an extended family and the grandeur of a pristine wilderness, and both played deeply on his character. His father, Archibald Stuart, was a noted Virginia politician, a fine singer and talented raconteur, though somewhat slack in managing family affairs. From Archibald's singing and storytelling came the origins of James' own conviviality. However, with his father gone much of the time, young James was educated at his mother's knee. A stern matriarch and devout Episcopalian, Elizabeth Stuart inculcated a strict code of personal morality, going so far as to elicit a lifetime oath from the twelve-year-old James to shun alcohol. Such puritanical stringency might have created a dullard, but the setting of Laurel Hill at the eastern foot of the Blue Ridge Mountains gave James the eye of an artist. He would later write of "the sweet Cape Jessamine that bloomed in the arbor" and "the grand and picturesque mountain scenery" of upstate New York. Nature could always enrapture the young man, whether in the wilds of west Texas, the flatlands of Kansas, or the war-torn Piedmont of Virginia.

A nature lover, yes, but still a boy with considerable spunk. One day the youngster and his brother William determined to destroy a hornets' nest by climbing a tree and striking it with sticks. When the operation came to grief in a swarm of angry insects, William abandoned his perch while his younger brother braved the stings and beat the nest until the mission was completed. Such determination would come in handy, for Laurel Hill burned down in the winter of 1847 and forced the dispersal of the Stuart family. Independent by nature, James Stuart was forced to become his own man at a very early age.

After some preliminary schooling near Wytheville, the fifteen year-old Stuart entered Emory & Henry College in nearby Washington County. There his interests expanded, but no scholarly subject matter struck the teenager as intensely as the Methodist revival that swept the campus his freshman year. From then on, James' personal relationship with his Redeemer became the cornerstone of his personality. Still, he developed a fiercely pragmatic side. Well aware there would be no great inheritance awaiting him, Stuart would write, "the young man for whom capital has not already been accumulated is forced to adopt one of the hireling professions..."Ironically, one of his father's failures helped create the

6

opportunity for James to pursue his life's work. In 1848 Archibald Stuart lost a Congressional election to Dr. Thomas Averett. According to tradition, Averett's first official action was to chivalrously appoint his opponent's son to the United States Military Academy.

Young Stuart left home in late May of 1850, stopping first at Monticello, the home of Thomas Jefferson, then travelling on to Washington D.C. He later made steamboat passage to New York City where, after a short stay, he moved on to the final leg of his journey. Sometime before midnight, surrounded by dark fastness of the Hudson River valley, Stuart disembarked onto the West Point pier. On July 1, 1850, he officially became a "plebe" and immediately embraced his surroundings, writing that "everything connected with the Academy has far surpassed my most sanguine expectations." At this point he was having no second thoughts about his chosen path: "So far I know of no profession more desirable than that of a soldier."

Very soon the West Point academic regimen forced Stuart to admit grudgingly, "I turned into studying pretty hard." The extra labor produced results, for at the end of his first year, he stood eighth in his class. The eighteen-year-old developed a formula for success at the Academy: "an ordinary mind and application," with application "by far the most important and desirable of the two." Stuart began his second year as corporal of the corps and serving then as the orderly sergeant for Company A during the summer encampment. His successes had him crowing to his cousin, "...I have been granted many privileges...so upon the whole I have had a splendid time." Additionally, he was quite pleased that cavalry drills had begun, noting that they were "great fun to us from the South." By the end of his second year, Corporal Stuart was regarded as one of the finest horsemen at the Point and stood to seventh in his class standing.

Ever gregarious, the rapidly maturing cadet made a number of good friends at the Point, including the similarly religious Oliver Otis Howard and George Washington Custis Lee, son of Mexican War hero Lieutenant Col. Robert E. Lee. One more thing: Stuart's weak, sloping chin had prompted his comrades to give him a nickname based upon "his personal comeliness in inverse ratio to the term employed." With ironic glee, James Stuart's fellow cadets were now addressing him as "Beauty."

In the summer after his second year, Stuart spent the ten weeks of his furlough visiting family and friends. The sojourn intensified James' love of his native state, as the cadet now pined for "warmhearted Virginians" and commented on "the superiority of our Virginia girls." Concurrently, an emerging sectionalism crept into his own correspondence: his awareness of the "taint" of "free-soil-Yankeedom," and his relief that "A majority of the officers and professors (at West Point) are from the south." However, when a cabal of Southern cadets conspired to shun the ultra-Northern abolitionist Oliver Howard, "Beauty" warmly befriended him. Years later, Howard would write, "I never can forget the manliness of J. E. B. Stuart."

In Stuart's third year, the corps had a new commander. Col. Robert E. Lee had arrived to superintend West Point, and, through his friendship with Custis Lee, Stuart quickly became part of the inner circle. The increased socializing didn't affect his class standing, however. James managed to keep his grades up through his final two years at the Point, eventually graduating thirteenth in his class. Family tradition held that James purposely fell in class rank to avoid assignment to the engineers. Whatever the reason, the young man was appointed one of eight cavalry officers and was accorded the honor of being named second captain of the corps. His conduct, however, never quite matched his classroom and drill field accomplishments. Fitzhugh Lee recalled Stuart's "almost thankful acceptance of a challenge from any cadet to fight." Indeed, his total of 129 demerits in four years at the Point placed him exactly in the middle of the pack.

Two matters pressed heavily upon James Stuart his last year at West Point. His father's body and mind had begun to fail, and tax records of the time suggest that Jeb's parents were maintaining separate residences. Also, Stuart was now re-thinking his career choices—"the important crisis"—and he discussed his options with his family and friends. Writing his father, he perceived but two directions, "the profession of arms and that of law." To his cousin Bettie Hairston, however, James saw the choice a simple one: "(H)ad you not rather see your cousin...a bold dragoon than a petty-fogger lawyer?" Upon his graduation, Stuart requested active duty, and, after a summer of travelling and visiting, received his orders. He was now a Brevet Second Lieutenant James Stuart of the Mounted Riflemen, assigned to the wilds of Texas.

THE FRONTIER WEST

Lieutenant Stuart reached Fort Davis near the Texas town of Limpia on January 29, 1855. In his first patrol into Indian country, he was given command of a single artillery piece which he managed to manhandle down a "stupendous precipice" to the amazement of his commander, Major John Simonson. As the column progressed, Stuart found the duty difficult and the elements harsh, but the young Lieutenant appeared to revel in the hardships. He also decided to grow a "flourishing" beard which he admitted "has so much altered my physique that you could not recognize me." One officer present who knew "Beauty" back at the Point agreed, describing Stuart as "the only man he ever saw that a beard improved."

But, James' stay on the Texas frontier was brief. In the winter of 1855, Secretary of War Jefferson Davis had authorized the creation of the 1st and 2nd United States Cavalry, elite units designed to operate against the plains Indians. Stuart was thrilled to learn that, as of March 3, he had been made 2nd Lieutenant in the 1st U.S. Cavalry. In June he moved to his new post, Fort Leavenworth in the Kansas Territory where he was given a multiple assignment as regimental quartermaster, assistant commisary officer, and post treasurer. Here he found himself in the company of the some of the Army's finest officers. Col. Edwin Sumner commanded Stuart's new unit, with Joseph E. Johnston serving as Lieutenant Colonel. Very soon the gregarious 2nd Lieutenant had made the aquaintance of the post's remaining officers, including the colonel of the nearby 2nd U.S. Dragoons, an esteemed cavalryman named Philip St. George Cooke. Of all his acquaintances in Kansas, this last would be the most significant.

On August 10, 1855, James wrote his cousin. "(S)ome seven or eight ladies can always hoist sail for amusement. I have been riding with one nearly every suitable evening since I went up." With these words, J.E.B. Stuart announced his yielding to Cupid's demands. Her name was Flora Cooke, and by late September, James and the young woman were engaged to be married. The attraction seemed most natural. She could ride a horse, shoot a gun, and enliven a party with her music. He was an

Note: In the text of an unpublished Stuart biography, his wife Flora stated that her husband was given the name "Jeb" in 1855 ["when he became a Lieut. in 1st U.S. Cavalry—to distinguish him from Lieut. 'Geo. H. Stewart.'"]

Ambrotype of J.E.B. Stuart as West Point cadet ca. 1854. *Museum of the Confederacy*

Pre-war daguerretype of Flora Cooke Stuart, probably taken at the time of her marriage. *Library of Virginia*

Army "comer," gifted ahorse and dashing to boot. "Veni, Vidi, Victus sum," was James' description of the short and swift campaign. Conquered he was, by the Colonel's daughter.

Despite news of the death of Archibald Stuart—which prompted Jeb to write "how difficult it is to realize such a heartrending occurrence...Alas! What a shadow is life!"—wedding preparations continued apace. On November 14, 1855, James Stuart and Flora Cooke were married, a union that would last eight and a half years and produce three children. From testimony on all sides, few Civil War era marriages were as happy as theirs.

After a short visit to Virginia, the couple returned to Kansas where Jeb found himself promoted to first Lieutenant. "Tumultuous" best describes Kansas in 1856, and Indian trouble seemed the very least of the territory's problems. With statehood looming, Kansas had become a battleground pitting free-soilers against proponents of the peculiar institution, often with deadly results. After a clash near an outpost called Black Jack, Stuart accompanied a cavalry column into the free-soil camp where he met Captain John Brown, one of the more violent abolitionists of his time. Stuart thought little of the affair, but the meeting would set the stage for a later, far more explosive encounter.

In December, Flora discovered she was pregnant. Despite the joyous tidings, darkness loomed. Cheyenne war parties were terrorizing settlers in the western reaches of the territory, and in May of 1857, Col. Sumner was ordered to lead a large column from Fort Leavenworth to chastise the marauders. Although Stuart had been relieved of his quartermaster duties, Sumner thought enough of the Lieutenant to assign him command of Company G, his first command in the field.

After two months of the chase, Stuart finally came face to face with the enemy. When Sumner's force made contact with 300 Cheyenne warriors, the Colonel immediately deployed his six cavalry companies for action. As the army charged with sabers drawn, the Indians broke ranks and fled. Stuart galloped in pursuit for five miles, riding up just as three of his comrades had cornered an armed Cheyenne. As the horsemen closed on him, the Indian fired pointblank at the mounted officer, his bullet slamming deeply into James' chest beneath the left nipple.

Luckily, the wound was more painful than life-threatening and Stuart was assured of a complete recovery. Since Sumner decided to continue the pursuit of the Indians, the incapacitated Lieutenant was left with medical staff in a rough field fortification under the protection of a single cavalry company. Here he lay for six days until Sumner's Pawnee scouts arrived bringing word of the Colonel's orders to return to Fort Kearny.

Departing on August 8, the small command made only modest headway, being hindered by the lack of a compass. Then, on August 14, disaster struck. In a thick fog, the Pawnee scouts vanished, throwing the troopers on their own. In such an emergency, Stuart acted decisively, volunteering to take a small party and locate Fort Kearny. For three days, the wounded Stuart combated thick fog, violent storm, and a flash flood that nearly drowned the entire command to lead his ragged column to Fort Kearney. Nonetheless, with a bullet in his chest and nature on the rampage, Stuart brought his boys in safely.

In early September, 1857, Jeb Stuart became father to a baby girl named Flora. Soon thereafter, the 1st Cavalry was ordered west to Fort Riley where the Stuarts set up family housekeeping. For the next several months, he and elements of the 1st Cavalry bounced between Forts Riley and Scott on simple policing expeditions, while participating in an aborted move to support the "Utah Forces." In his spare time, he studied law and passed an exam, while designing both a cavalry "horse hitcher" and an improved brass belt attachment for saber and scabbard. His efforts as an inventor paid off. In 1859 he was granted six months leave to come east to patent his products and negotiate their sale. Which he did. In September Stuart brought his family to Virginia and journeyed to Washington to hammer out an agreement for his inventions. After a few days of haggling the War Department agreed to pay $5000 for the right to produce his belt attachment.

HARPER'S FERRY

The morning of October 17 found Jeb at the War Department awaiting a meeting with Secretary of War John Floyd, when he heard that a mob of three thousand slaves had taken over a Federal Arsenal at Harper's Ferry. He immediately volunteered his services to the Secretary, and was dispatched to inform Colonel Robert E. Lee (like Stuart, also home on leave) of the situation at the Ferry and to accompany Lee to the scene of the revolt. Jeb "had barely time to borrow a uniform coat and a sabre," but he and Lee managed to board a waiting train and ride west towards the crisis.

The two officers reached Harper's Ferry sometime before midnight. Awaiting them was a force of Marines commanded by Lieutenant Israel Green, who informed Lee that the insurgent "mob" was in fact a rather small group led by a man named "Smith" which had barricaded itself in a nearby engine house. After relieving the militiamen with the Marines, Lee formulated his plans. To safeguard the hostages, he decided to delay action until morning. At daybreak, Stuart would deliver an untimatum to surrender. If the demand was rejected—as Lee assumed it would be—Stuart was to wave his hat signalling the assault. Lee wrote out the orders around 2:00 am; afterwhich, in a cold drizzle, he and Stuart hunkered down to await the sunrise.

Around 7:00 am, the principals gathered. Stuart and Green approached the engine house. Behind them stood twenty-four Marines. Lee stood off on a rise, observing the operation with dignified calm. Around the actors had gathered perhaps two thousand spectators. When Stuart reached the heavy wooden doors, he announced that he had a communication for Smith from Colonel Lee. The door opened perhaps four inches, and Jeb found himself looking down the business end of a "cocked carbine." Behind the gun stood John Brown whom Jeb remembered well. Stuart explained the terms for Brown's surrender, but the rebel leader asked that his raiding party be allowed to leave. Although Stuart expected as much, he was struck by Brown's "admirable tact." As the tet-a-tete dragged on, the hostages began to call out for Lee himself to come in to see them. Above their croaking rose the voice of Lewis Washington, a descendant of the first President, which implored, "Never mind us, fire!" Jeb then stepped back from the building with a wave of his cap.

The resulting melee lasted perhaps three minutes, as the Marines used a ladder to batter a small opening in the door. Green wriggled in and fell upon Brown, slashing and raining blows about his head. The soldiers behind mopped up quickly, bayoneting two of the insurgents and capturing two others, while freeing all the hostages. As Lee and Stuart approached the building, some of the Marines were dragging the unconscious Brown out of the engine house. Stuart now informed Lee that Mr. Smith was, in fact, John Brown of "Bleeding Kansas" fame. Brown would say he could have wiped Stuart out like a mosquito when they met at the doorway, but Jeb was unmoved, later remarking that his razor-sharp sabre "would have saved Virginia the expense of Brown's trial." Stuart then led a Marine contingent to Brown's hideout where they found close to 1600 pikes. Over the next few days he would act as Lee's aide-

13

de-camp, delivering orders and policing the surroundings. Finally, with the prisoners remanded to the U.S. Marshall, Lee, Stuart, and the Marines departed.

Despite the handsome business deal he had struck, the Harper's Ferry business left Stuart in an anxious state. The public reaction to John Brown's raid prompted him to plead with Virginia's Governor Wise to organize and outfit more militia companies. With the state in an "exposed position...to attack from the North," well-regulated militias were now a necessity. The storm clouds were ominuous, and Stuart feared for his beloved Virginia.

By Christmas, however, he was back at Fort Riley. Although his family was thriving, Jeb was now concerned with being isolated in the wilderness. In May, he joined an Indian expedition that would keep him in the field for some three months. Returning in August, he found a new son waiting for him, a boy he and Flora named Phillip St. George Cooke Stuart to honor Flora's father. Within a few weeks he left for Fort Wise, a primitive post almost 400 miles west of Fort Riley. Even more isolated, he could barely keep up with the emerging secession crisis. But, beginning in December, as one Southern state after the other seceeded from the Union to form the Confederate States of America, Stuart began corresponding with a number of prominent Southerners, assuring them where he stood: "(R)ight or wrong, alone or otherwise, I go with Virginia..."

1861

On January 11, 1861, Lt. Stuart retired to Fort Riley to "await the march of events" with his family. As the secession crisis deepened, Jeb received leave and made his way east. On April 17, following Fort Sumter's fall and President Abraham Lincoln's call for volunteers, the Virginia State Convention voted to seceed from the United States. After pausing briefly in St. Louis, Stuart and family boarded a steamer for Memphis. Stopping in Cairo, Illinois, Jeb mailed off two letters, one to Virginia state Adjutant General Samuel Cooper requesting a command in the new Confederate Army, the other to the U.S. Army announcing his resignation: "From a sense of duty to my native State Virginia, I hereby resign my position as an officer in the Army of the United States."

On May 10, 1861, Stuart received a Virginia infantry commission, and left immediately to join the command of Colonel Thomas J. Jackson

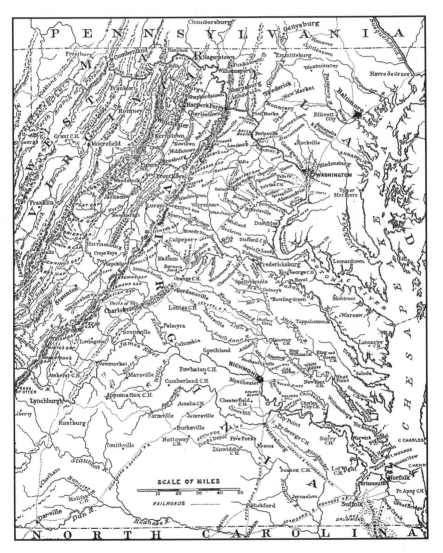

Robert U. Johnson and Clarence C Buel, eds. Battles and Leaders of the Civil War. (New York: The Century Co. 1887-88), Vol. 1, 121.

at Harper's Ferry. He would serve under Jackson for only two weeks, but during this time Jackson made a decision that would dramatically shape the course of Stuart's wartime career. When Captain Turner Ashby led a collection of undisciplined cavalrymen into camp, Jackson sensed trouble. To keep the peace, the Colonel divided his cavalry companies, sending half with Ashby to patrol the Potomac while re-organizing the other half under Stuart. Thanks to Jackson, Stuart was out of the infantry and once again in his natural role as a cavalryman.

In late May, Joseph E. Johnston arrived to supercede Jackson, and immediately ordered a retreat to Winchester, Virginia. Stuart set up camp some miles north of Winchester near the hamlet of Bunker Hill. "(H)ere all looked like business," said one eyewitness of the scene, for Jeb Stuart was turning volunteers into troopers. He had become a Colonel on May 24, and, at age 28, he certainly looked the part, "a little above medium height, broad shouldered and powerfully built, ruddy complexion and blue-gray eyes..." There was an extra verve to Stuart that made a lasting impression on the recruits. Volunteers trickling in to Camp Jeff Davis learned quickly that cavalry life with Stuart would be active, demanding, and exciting—usually all at once.

For example, Jeb would lead his men into Federal lines and allow the Yankees to surround them, then calmly guide them out. He would boldly parade his squadrons before the enemy to provoke cannon fire, and then, when the fire came, remark with a laugh that "I wanted you to learn what a cannon's like, and hear it." But above all, he would demand that his cavalry gallop at the Yankees and always, always trot away, for a "good man on a horse need never get in trouble." Under Stuart's watchful eye, his 1st Virginia Cavalry was quickly becoming the South's premier mounted unit.

Early July brought stirrings from the North, as General Robert Patterson began crossing Federal forces over the Potomac. Jackson and Stuart fought a sharp little delaying action with Patterson's vanguard at Falling Waters. During the course of the fight, the Stuart legend began. Well in advance of his command, Jeb found himself facing a full company of Yankees lining a fence in a field. All alone, he simply ordered the Bluecoats to throw down the fence then pulled his pistol and announced their capture—to forty-six stunned soldiers from the 15th Pennsylvania, who did as they were told.

In mid-July, Johnston's 11,000 troops prepared to move east. A large Federal force under General Irwin McDowell had marched out of

Washington towards General P.G.T. Beauregard's 20,000 men near Manassas. To reinforce Beauregard, Richmond ordered Johnston to Piedmont Station for transportation by rail to Manassas. Stuart was ordered to mask the movement and how well he did his job is reflected in Patterson's absolute ignorance of Johnston's manuever. On July 18, Johnston commenced the transfer of his entire command over the Blue Ridge. Once the Confederate infantry had departed Winchester, Stuart ordered part of his command to pester Patterson and led the rest eastward. Thirty-six bone-wearying hours later, near sundown on the 20th, Jeb Stuart led the 1st Virginia Cavalry into Manassas.

The following morning, at first light, small arms fire erupted towards the Confederate left. "Hello! What is that?" Stuart asked to no one in particular. He immediately ordered his men on a scout across Bull Run, but the troopers met no enemy. Even as the roar of battle trebled to the north and west, the only orders Stuart received were those detaching two of his companies for service elsewhere. Observing the progress of the battle, he spent the rest of the morning and early afternoon nervously awaiting orders and pacing furiously about.

Around 2:00 pm, Beauregard summoned Stuart's horsemen, admonishing the cavalry to "attack where the firing is hottest." Jeb led the 1st Virginia to the sound of the guns, entering the "grand panorama" of battle on the Confederate left. Seventy yards to their front, the New York Fire Zouaves and the 14th New York were turning out of the deep depression of the Sudley Springs Road and trying to counter Jackson's Virginians on nearby Henry House Hill. Stuart turned to a nearby aide and asked if the Zouaves were in fact Confederates. When the appearance of the Stars and Stripes resolved the matter, Jeb ordered his rearmost troopers to oblique to the left, wheeled his horse and called for an attack. The Zouaves saw the charge coming and managed to fire off a volley just as the Virginians thundered into their ragged formation. Once past the Yankees, Stuart redirected his troopers back through the New Yorkers to safety. Again the two forces hacked and shot at each other. This time, however, many of the Virginians needed to be corralled back into position, much to their commander's chagrin.

Once reformed, Stuart's regiment took up a post of observation on Chinn Ridge near Lt. Robert Beckham's artillery battery. From there Jeb effectively directed Beckham's fire and kept other infantry commanders informed of Federal movements. Around 4:00 pm, the cavalryman became convinced that the Federal right was about to crumble. He sent word to Col. Jubal Early to press his brigade against the teetering enemy positions. Early advanced his columns while Stuart and Beckham struck at the Union flank. Suddenly the rout was on. Stuart's men swept the battlefield, reining in so many Yankees that the 1st Virginia mired down in shepherding prisoners to the rear. With the sun setting and the enemy streaming back towards Washington, a jovial Jeb Stuart set up headquarters near the Sudley Church.

THE GENERAL

On July 23, Stuart advanced to Fairfax Court House and promptly established Camp Qui Vive ("Who goes there?"), where began another round of training and outpost duty. One eyewitness reported that the Colonel "lived nearly all the time between the picket lines of the two armies," and his superiors took note. Concurring with James Longstreet and P.G.T. Beauregard, General Joseph Johnston advised Jefferson Davis that Stuart was "a rare man...If you add a brigade of cavalry to this army, you cannot find a better brigadier-general to command it."

Myriad stories detailing Jeb's bravado made the rounds that summer, but one above all seemed to catch the true spirit of the youthful commander. While admiring a courier's horse, Jeb offered to switch mounts and go for a ride. The two cantered past the furthest Confederate outpost then took to the fields and woods. The courier soon became alarmed, well aware that they had penetrated enemy lines, but Stuart airily dismissed the danger. As they regained the road, both men spurred their horses to a gallop and streaked past the startled Federal pickets. By the time the videttes discharged their rifles, the Southrons were one hundred yards away. Stuart remained quiet on the return ride but in camp asked the trooper if he had ever timed the animal over a half-mile.

Many would criticize the Stuart style, but there was a method to the man in the early days of the war that bears serious analysis. He commanded some of Virginia's finest horsemen, themselves a high-spirited lot, and volunteers to boot. Establishing discipline under such circumstances proved a formidable task for even the best of officers, but, leading by example, Stuart seems to have had little trouble gaining their allegiance. At the same time, Stuart was conceiving a new, patently more aggressive approach to the use of cavalry, and he stressed the importance of esprit de corps in molding this new type of cavalry arm. Like Jackson's "foot cavalry," Stuart's men would follow their commander anywhere—"He leads us-he don't send us." The "old-liners" may have frowned upon the singing, but they couldn't argue with the results. His superiors certainly liked what they saw; on September 24, the Confederate War Department consolidated Johnston's six regiments of cavalry into a brigade under newly-commisioned Brigadier General James Ewell Brown Stuart.

In the autumn of 1861, Camp Qui Vive came to epitomise the Stuart style. The farmhouse headquarters may have had a stark, military air; but Jeb collected musicians with his facile touch, and the place literally echoed with song. Sam Sweeny arrived with his banjo and became Stuart's personal "gleeman." Stuart's servant Bob joined in on the bones. However, the serious business of war demanded a dedicated, diligent staff, and Stuart hand-picked his supporting cast with unerring insight. Jeb tabbed John Pelham to command the horse artillery, and young Pelham would respond by practically rewriting the manual. John Mosby, a frail lawyer from the Virginia uplands, arrived on an errand one day; Stuart immediately took him under his wing. Before the war was over, Mosby would become the guerilla leader nonpareil. They knew how to enjoy themselves, these men of Qui Vive, but they also learned well how to fight a war, Jeb Stuart-style.

In late December, Jeb was assigned a mixed force to protect a foraging expedition operating near the town of Dranesville. On the 20th, he moved forward but found the area crawling with Bluecoats. Outnumbered yet recognizing the danger to the trains, Stuart was forced to deploy on unfavorable ground and watch his artillery suffer under severe counter-battery fire. His infantry could do little better in the heavily wooded terrain. Despite rather heavy casualties of 194—including 43 killed—Stuart managed not only to bring off the trains and but also to personally remove an artillery harness from the battlefield.

As his legend grew, some of Stuart's higher ranking subordinates began grousing among themselves. Colonel William E. "Grumble" Jones of the 1st Virginia Cavalry held a deep-seated dislike for the General that pre-dated the war. Beverly Robertson, colonel of the 4th Virginia Cavalry, drew Stuart's ire by being "the most troublesome man" he had to deal with. What's more, Stuart could sense "a good deal of envy in the army," but he let its presence trouble him "precious little." Drill had turned his brigade into a splendid fighting force. What did trouble him intensely was the failure of his father-in-law to come over to the Confederacy. Philip St. George Cooke was now a Federal cavalry General, and, in retaliation, Stuart ordered Flora to change their son's name. As for the elder Cooke's choice of armies, Jeb proclaimed, "He will regret it but once and that will be continually."

Stuart could also see the war's emerging dark course. Running beneath his surface gaiety was a deeply fatalistic streak. He once remarked, "(T)he war is going to be a long and terrible one...and very few of us will see the end." Yet, through these stark realizations, Jeb had his Flora. He wrote to her of a life far removed from the battlefield, with "a little home...somewhere to have birds and flowers and books. When 'war's dread commotion is over,' I would step quietly into such a home and xxxxxxxxxx." He signed the reverie, "Kisses Dearest—your own—Stuart."

1862

With the coming of spring, the Army of the Potomac stirred from its winter camps, leaving Joe Johnston in a quandary. To guard against either an overland assault or a sea-based attack against Richmond, the Confederate commander thought it better to abandon Centreville and retreat towards Culpeper. Jeb Stuart did not share Johnston's uncertainty over the enemy's course, announcing that "we shall hear of him (McClellan) presently on his way up the James River." On March 9 the withdrawal began. Poorly conceived and badly managed, the evacuation cost the Confederacy mountains of unmoveable supplies. Stuart screened the retreat and found the movement terribly depressing. However, he bolstered himself by proclaiming to Flora, "We must plant our feet firmly upon the platform of our inextinguishable hatred for the Northern Confederacy, with a determination to die rather than submit."

McClellan eventually got his army ashore at Fortress Monroe, at the tip of the Virginia Peninsula, and forced Johnston to cover Richmond. Arriving near Yorktown on April 18, Stuart realized that the terrain was unfavorable to cavalry action, but he knew his boys would prove their worth in gathering intelligence. When Johnston abandoned Yorktown on May 3, Stuart divided his command into three battalions and screened the Confederate retreat. Fitzhugh Lee's regiment helped repulse a Federal thrust at Eltham's Landing, but Confederate disarray elsewhere left Stuart himself surrounded. With characteristic aplomb, he simply trotted south to the James River and made his escape by using its beach as a roadway.

On May 5, Johnston fought a delaying action near the historic town of Williamsburg, but, within two weeks, the armies were facing off near the outskirts of Richmond. On May 31, at the Battle of Seven Pines, General Joseph Johnston was incapacitated by a stray cannon shot. The next day, General Robert E. Lee became commander of the Confederate army and promptly renamed it the Army of Northern Virginia. Though Stuart truly respected his new commander, he had once written that Lee "has disappointed me as a general." His opinion would soon change.

RIDING A RAID

Soon after Lee took charge, Stuart proposed attacking Little Mac's left. Lee rejected the idea but considered ordering the cavalry on a reconnaissance towards the Union right. Jubilant to be leading such a raid, Stuart confidently informed Lee that he could pass around McClellan's entire army. On the next day, June 11th, Lee's orders for Stuart urged caution, placing intelligence and wagon-hunting above "all that might be desired." Stuart in turn issued his troopers 60 rounds and alerted them to prepare three days of rations.

Around 2 a.m. on June 12, to the tune of Sam Sweeney's banjo, Stuart's 1200-man column swung out from their camps north of Richmond and trotted up the Brook Turnpike. Passing Old Yellow Tavern, they angled left on the Mountain Road and crossed the Richmond, Fredricksbug & Potomac Railroad. As they rode, word quickly spread that the force was headed for Shenandoah Valley and Stonewall Jackson's Army. But, six miles later Stuart—"the perfect picture of a gay cavalier"—led the horsemen east on the Hughes Road and recrossed the railroad, finally camping beyond the Brook Turnpike near Winston's farm. Here the men quietly bedded down, well aware that this wasn't the road to the Shenandoah Valley.

Early the next morning, the column pressed east towards Hanover Court House where scouts spotted Union cavalry. Stuart determined to catch the Yankees in a pincers, but Fitz Lee was delayed by a swamp and never made his blocking position. By the time Stuart entered the town, the Yanks had escaped south. However, a second Federal patrol advancing from the east spied the Confederates and quickly withdrew. Assuming now that word of their presence deep in Yankee territory would spread, Jeb guided the column onto a side road. Just beyond Haw's Shop, skirmishers of the 9th Virginia Cavalry engaged a dawdling Federal patrol, but Stuart arrived to order a saber charge that cleared the road to the Totopotomoy Bridge. Rooney Lee's aggressiveness convinced

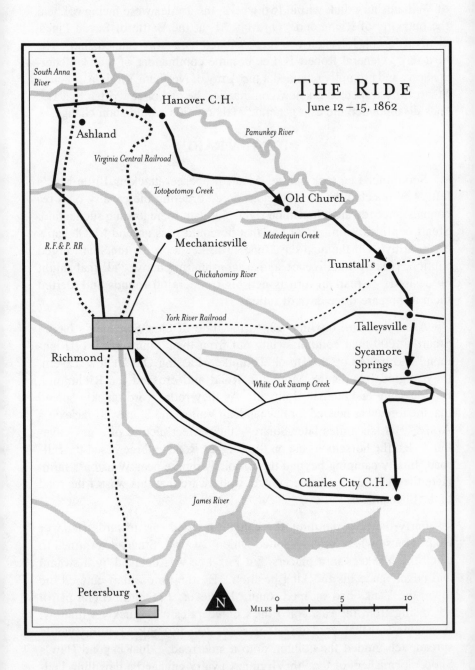

THE RIDE

June 12–15, 1862

South Anna River

Hanover C.H.

Ashland

Pamunkey River

Virginia Central Railroad

Totopotomoy Creek

Old Church

R.F.&P. RR

Mechanicsville

Matedequin Creek

Chickahominy River

Tunstall's

York River Railroad

Talleysville

Richmond

Sycamore Springs

White Oak Swamp Creek

Charles City C.H.

James River

Petersburg

N

MILES 0 5 10

the Federals that the game was up, and presently the enemy was in full retreat down the road towards Old Church.

It was now mid-afternoon. The Confederates pressed the Federals towards Old Church until Stuart's vanguard came upon a column of Union cavalry deployed four abreast with sabers drawn. The Confederate skirmishers fell back, but Jeb arrived with the 9th Virginia and ordered a charge. Captain William Latane led his boys into the teeth of the Federal formation. Amidst the saber slashings and pistol shots, Latane was killed by a Yankee captain, but the Confederates cleared the road and pushed on to Old Church. After a brief Yankee stand, Fitz Lee ran the last Union cavalry outfit out of the village. With the locals cheering their heroes, Jeb Stuart had reached his objective in fine style. If there was a decision to be made concerning the route back, Jeb made it quickly. Late that afternoon, Stuart led his men south towards the Chickahominy.

As the column approached the road to Garlick's Landing on the Pamunkey, Stuart detached two squads to capture enemy stores. Meanwhile, the Confederates brushed back a Yankee patrol and swept into Tunstall's Station on the Richmond & York RR, scattering the Federal defenders. Then, just as Confederate troopers were severing telegraph lines and blocking the tracks, a Union supply train came roaring through. Although one trooper managed to kill the engineer, the locomotive sped on. White House Landing and its immense stores were just five inviting miles east of Tunstall's, and Stuart had another decision to make. Realizing that the Landing would be heavily defended, and that Yankee pursuit certainly would be intensifying, he reluctantly headed his men south.

The column made Talleysville around 8:30 pm where a halt was called. For nearly four hours the troopers rested, but by midnight, they were back in their saddles winding enroute to the Chickahominy. During this leg of the journey, even the General himself succumbed to the need for sleep. But, up ahead was a hidden ford that could be used if the Forge Bridge had been destroyed. Daylight, however, revealed both the bridge in ruins and the ford flooded and unsafe. When asked of the predicament, a dispirited Rooney Lee admitted, "I think we are caught," but his chief was having none of it. He quickly led the column east to the site of the Forge Bridge and ordered work parties to repair the damaged structure. Crews tore down a nearby barn and fashioned a rough pontoon bridge anchored near the bridge's abuttments. Half the command managed to cross the swaying planks, but Jeb needed a faster process.

Another barn fell to the straining Confederates, but this time the heavy timbers were laid on the abutments and flooring was quickly secured. Although the men expected "at every instant an overpowering force of the enemy," the voice of Jeb Stuart floated above the operation "singing carelessly". By 1:00 pm, the last Confederate crossed the bridge. When John Esten Cooke later observed that their options had been very nearly limited to surrender, Stuart replied that there had been another: "To die game."

With his horsemen safely across and bedded down, Stuart and two orderlies trotted all night, mostly through enemy-held territory, to arrive at Lee's headquarters in Richmond at sunup. Soon thereafter, his main body entered Confederate lines near New Market Heights. The troopers leisurely made their way to their camps north of Richmond, having completed the 100-mile "Ride Around McClellan."

Stuart gave Lee exactly what the General needed: detailed intelligence of both McClellan's rear and right flank. He could also claim capturing 164 Yanks and 260 of their horses and mules, besides destroying the Tunstall's depot. Some argue that the ride alerted Little Mac to the dangers of his position and hastened his change of base to the James River. But, most glorious was the effect of the ride on Stuart's men in particular and Lee's army in general. Where as days before, a gloom had pervaded the Confederate defenders, there was now a belief that "We are going to whip the Yankees like the mischief." Jeb was now being feted in the streets of Richmond while McClellan was being lampooned in the North.

SEVEN DAYS

With Stuart's report in hand, Robert E. Lee unleashed his counterstroke. First, Lee summoned Stonewall Jackson and his "foot cavalry" from their own myth-making campaign in the Shenandoah Valley. Concurrently, Lee ordered Stuart to cover Jackson's approach and guide the infantry into place. With his typical efficiency, Jeb secured the proposed route to the Federal flank before rendezvousing with Stonewall on June 26 near Ashland. However, as Stuart and his men fanned out before the advance, the vaunted but exhausted Valley Army simply trudged listlessly to camp. While Lee's men attacked the isolated Federals, a spent Stonewall Jackson determined that he had done all that he could that day. Stuart dutifully picketed the encampment, while, at the town of Mechanicsville just three miles away, Lee's troops fought and died for another four hours.

On June 22, Stuart protected Jackson's flank on the march to Gaines Mill. After a day of piecemeal assaults, Lee finally marshalled his forces and delivered a late afternoon attack that pierced the Federal lines and drove the Yankees south of the Chickahominy. All the while, Stuart stalked the front, looking for opportunities to send in his troopers. Despite the carnage, Jeb retained his good humor. At one point, when brother-in-law John Esten Cooke fell from his horse to avoid an artillery shell, Jeb inquired if the Captain had been injured. "Oh, no, General; I only dodged a little too far," was his sheepish reply. Stuart roared with laughter and for months after would greet Cooke in the morning with the question, "Hello Cooke! Are you hit?"

The next day, Lee called his commanders to a morning meeting at D. H. Hill's headquarters, the McGehee house. There, Stuart learned that he and General Richard S. Ewell were to attack the Federal supply base at White House Landing for the purpose of drawing a response that would reveal McClellan's plans. While at McGehee's, Jeb found Hill's copy of Lee's orders for the pursuit of McClellan lying on the floor. After taking measures to return the documents to Lee's careless divisional commander, Stuart set out for the Pamunkey. His command reached Tunstall's Station on the Richmond and York line before it encountered serious opposition, making possible the report that Little Mac had abandoned the railroad supply line and was retreating south to the James. The bridge crossing at Black Creek lay in ruins, and a modest enemy force held the opposite bank. Stuart's troopers cleared the opposition, allowing the engineers to rebuild the bridge, but it was dark before the men could cross. However, as the sun set and darkness descended, the sky to the east glowed red. The Federal depot at White House Landing was burning.

At first light on the 29th, Stuart and Rooney Lee's command trotted to the Landing and found a scene of mass destruction, including the charred remains of Rooney's house. Jeb spent the balance of the day confiscating what he could while destroying what remained. On the 30th, he detailed a regiment to guard the Landing and led the rest of his command south to link up with Jackson, but it wasn't until July 2 that Jeb located the left of Lee's army. He had missed Marse Robert's bloody attempts to corner the Federal army during McClellan's "change of base" to the James River, including the Confederate rebuff at Malvern Hill on

July 1.

In the morning fog of the 2nd, Jeb and Stonewall were conferring when engineer William Blackford reported the enemy positions atop Malvern abandoned. Stuart's men immediately took off after the retreating Bluecoats, and, during the night of the 2nd, John Pelham reported his discovery of the Federal camp at Harrison's Landing. What's more, the Yanks had not invested a plateau that dominated the area, and the young cannoneer requested additional artillery to fortify the place. The next morning, Stuart reported the opportunity to Jackson then set out for the front.

When Jeb crowned the Heights around 9:00 am, he saw McClellan's entire army lounging across the lowlands along the James River. Mistakenly assuming that Longstreet was at hand, Stuart ordered Pelham to open with his one serviceable gun. Soon, screaming shells were scattering the surprised Yankees, but the Federals eventually brought up artillery of their own. By 2:00 pm, Stuart was forced to withdraw from Evelington with Longstreet still six miles away. "I had the infinite gratification of slipping around to the enemy's rear and shelling his camp at Westover," he would proudly write to Flora, adding that, "If the Army had been up with me we would have finished the business."

DEADLY ADVENTURE

On the 25th, Jeb Stuart was promoted to Major General in command of a cavalry division. Fitz Lee now headed much of Stuart's old brigade, and Wade Hampton—the richest man in South Carolina and one of the wealthiest in the south—arrived to command a second brigade. More problematic would be the arrival of Turner Ashby's men. Ashby had been killed in the Valley, and Jefferson Davis assigned his former troops to Stuart's nemesis, Beverly Robertson. Along with Ashby's men came another perennial thorn in Jeb's side, "Grumble" Jones. Nevertheless, the 29 year old Major General was elated by his promotion and ripe for fresh adventures.

In the meanwhile, Washington had created the Army of Virginia out of a disparate group of independent commands and put westerner John Pope in charge. Concurrently, the Federal War Department called McClellan north to rendezvous with Pope's columns, but Little Mac petulantly delayed his departure. Sensing an opportunity, Lee dispatched

Stonewall Jackson's Corps to the north to crush Pope's vanguard. Savage fighting characterized the Confederate victory at Cedar Mountain on August 9, but Jackson eventually retreated through Gordonsville in an attempt to draw Pope's main force further south. Restrained by Washington, Pope instead camped north of the Rapidan and awaiting reinforcement by McClellan. When Little Mac finally began his withdrawal, Lee ordered a full concentration on Jackson to attack Pope before McClellan could arrive.

On the 17th, with Fitz Lee on the march, Lee ordered Stuart to circle Pope's left and destroy the bridge at Rappahanock Station while Lee's infantry moved west and attacked Pope's right and rear. If all went well, Pope would be trapped between the Rapidan and the Rappahannock. Stuart promised to trigger the movement on the morrow and dispatched two staff members to the hamlet of Verdiersville to await Fitz Lee's arrival. Spending the remainder of the day studying his surroundings, Stuart and his entourage—Von Borke, John Mosby, and an acquaintance named Gibson—arrived in Verdiersville, but Fitz Lee was nowhere to be seen. Highly miffed, Stuart sent his adjutant Norman Fitzhugh eastward to locate Fitz Lee's brigade, then joined his party on the porch of a nearby house and went to sleep.

Courier Fitzhugh travelled only a mile before he and his aide bedded down for the evening in an abandoned house. At dawn the pair were awakened by hoofbeats. Expecting the arrival of Fitz Lee's horsemen, they were startled to find themselves in the hands of a Federal cavalry patrol. The Yankee horsemen shook down the prisoners, capturing Lee's orders, then galloped west towards Verdiersville and a slumbering Jeb Stuart.

Hearing the approaching horsemen, Stuart and his staff roused themselves, fully expecting the tardy Fitz Lee. Mosby and Gibson were sent to meet them but hadn't travelled far before being met with pistol shots and curses. With Gibson and Mosby sounding the alarm, Stuart's party mounted their horses in a frantic rush. A hatless Jeb and Chiswell Dabney vaulted a fence, while Von Borke made his escape through an open gate in "(a) shower of carbine and pistol bullets." "I had a very narrow escape...," Jeb would relievedly write, but his personal belongings—including his prized plumed hat, haversack, and cloak—were now property of the Federal government. The shaken Confederates gathered in a woodlot about a mile away. Vowed Stuart, "I intend to make the Yankees pay for that hat."

Fitz Lee's misunderstanding of the need for celerity forced the rescheduling of the manuever. Even worse, the Federals now possessed the set of Lee's orders carried by Norman Fitzhugh. By the time the Confederates were ready to move, an alerted John Pope fell back across the Rappahannock. On the 20th, Stuart took up the hunt. Riding with Beverly Robertson's command, Jeb rousted Federal cavalry drawn up north of Brandy Station and chased them across the Rappahannock. While the cavalry spent the next day resting, Stuart cast about for fresh adventures. He proposed a raid on Catlett's Station in the Federal rear to General Lee. Within two hours, 1500 troopers and two guns were headed for the Rappahannock with orders to destroy the railroad bridge over Cedar Run and as much of the enemy communications as possible.

When his column arrived in Warrenton, Jeb learned that a local belle had bet a Yankee quartermaster a bottle of wine that the Northerner wouldn't get to Richmond in thirty days. Of course, if General Stuart could capture the cheeky Northerner and send him to Richmond as a prisoner, she would gladly pay off the bet. As severe storm broke over the column, the strike force departed Warrenton and angled towards Catlett's Station. As night fell—"The darkest night I ever saw," according to Jeb—the Confederates located a guide who promised to deliver them to Pope's camp. Inching up to the Federal depot, Stuart made his dispositions, then, with a bugle blast, the Confederate cavalry burst upon the unsuspecting Yankees.

Pope's camp erupted in a swirl of pandemonium. As panicky Federals scattered, fire exploded among the mountains of supplies, illuminating the depot with its wild reflection. Best of all, Stuart could claim Pope's uniform, dispatch book, and $520,000 in currency and gold. On the downside, the Confederates were unable to ignite the sodden Cedar Run bridge. But, as the horsemen cleared the station for the return home, Blackford discovered that one of his prisoners was the Yankee quartermaster who had made the bet with the Warrenton belle. When the column made Warrenton, Stuart transacted the debt payment to the delight of the citizenry. Back in camp on the 24th, Stuart showed Pope's uniform to anyone who would look, even eliciting a rare joke from Stonewall Jackson: "I believe I'd rather you had brought General Pope instead of his coat."

Stuart was thrilled with his raid, but Robert E. Lee regarded Stuart's efforts as gaining only some "minor advantage." Nonetheless, Pope's dispatch book revealed both the strength of Pope's forces and confirmed

Federal intentions to bring McClellan north. Up to this point, these were things Lee could only surmise, and now Stuart had provided the basis upon which Lee would fashion his new campaign to suppress the Federals. Best of all, in Jeb's mind, Pope's uniform squared the matter of his captured hat: "I have had my revenge out on Pope."

On the morning of the 25th, Stonewall Jackson and his 25,000 troops marched upriver, crossed the Rappahannock, and headed for Salem. Theareafter, Jeb's columns followed. By the time they reached Salem, the sun was up and Jackson's men were heading east. Stuart eventually connected with Jackson at Gainesville that afternoon. By evening, the Confederate cavalry had overrun Bristoe Station, nearly ten miles in John Pope's rear. A Federal train managed to blast through a rough barricade, but the Confederates threw a nearby switch and spectacularly derailed a second locomotive. Jackson then ordered Stuart north with Isaac Trimble's brigade to take Manassas Junction. Elements of Trimble's infantry captured some Union artillery before dawn, allowing Trimble to claim the depot for himself. Meanwhile, Jeb's dawn attack overwhelmed the Junction's defenders; suddenly Jackson's force was closer to Washington than Pope's own army.

On August 27, while Jackson's infantry helped themselves to Federal supplies at the Manassas Junction depot, Jeb Stuart was dispatching Fitz Lee to raise hell near Fairfax Court House and assigning Thomas Rosser and Thomas Mumford's regiments to march with Richard Ewell's infantry. He then spread an arc of pickets across Pope's front to monitor the Federal response to the raid. Finally, with his remaining horsemen, he helped Jackson's men fire Manassas Junction.

The next morning, as Jackson settled in along a ridge north and west of the battlefield of First Manassas, Stuart headed west with his small contingent to locate Longstreet and Lee. At Haymarket, however, Stuart ran into enemy infantry and spent the day skirmishing. He did manage to send Jackson's location to Lee who was just west of Thoroughfare Gap in the Bull Run Mountains. Although he could plainly observe Longstreet's assault on the Gap, Stuart was forced to return to Jackson after dark and had to postpone the attempted link-up with Lee until the next day. Meanwhile, Pope finally located Jackson and massed his forces for battle.

On the morning of August 29 as Pope launched his men at Jackson, Stuart again galloped west towards the Bull Run Mountains. Here he found Lee and Longstreet west of Gainesville with the long columns of

Robert E. Lee, *Valentine Museum*

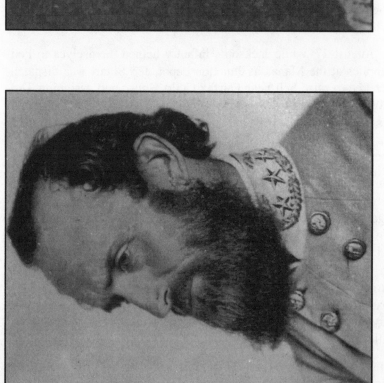

Thomas J. "Stonewall" Jackson, *Library of Congress*

The two legendary Confederate commanders most closely associated with J.E.B. Stuart.

Confederate infantry marching close behind. Thanks to Stuart's command of the terrain, Lee was able to put Longstreet in perfect position to support Jackson. However, as Stuart moved Beverly Robertson's brigade to protect Longstreet's right flank, trouble began developing on the cavalry front. Shocked to find a full Federal corps marching towards Longstreet's flank, Stuart immediately ordered his boys to drag pine boughs along the roadway and raise a dust cloud befitting an army on the march. In turn, Longstreet pushed infantry and artillery forward to confront the threat. After a number of exchanges, the Federals—Fitz John Porter's Fifth Corps—gingerly withdrew, ending the crisis. All that day, Pope threw his brigades at Jackson's position, with little if anything to show for the bloodshed.

At some point in the afternoon, Lee asked Jeb to await orders, prompting the cavalry commander to lay down on the ground to sleep. Returning an hour later, Lee asked for Stuart, whereupon Jeb "sprang to his feet and said, 'Here I am, General.'" Lee had a message for the outposts, but Stuart thought the General better served if he did it himself, "so he swung himself into the saddle and rode off at a rapid gallop, singing as loud as he could, 'Jine the cavalry.'" Recalling the moment, James Longstreet, would flatly assert that "'Jeb' Stuart was...the best cavalryman America ever produced."

Longstreet spent the balance of the 29th and most of the 30th arranging his brigades on Jackson's right flank. Finally, near 3:00 pm, he unleashed them. When Longstreet's troops swept forward, Pope's men could do little but fight a series of desperate delaying actions all the way back to Bull Run. In the meantime, Stuart ordered Robertson to advance on Longstreet's right in hopes of flanking the enemy and gaining the Warrenton Turnpike—Pope's escape route—well to the rear. Robertson advanced slowly but reached the high ground just south of Lewis Ford when he contacted Federal horse. But, instead of staying true to form and dispersing, the enemy beat back Robertson's first foray and forced the Confederates to marshall their full force. Eventually, Robertson rocked the Federals back, but his pursuit gained little advantage, and darkness finally ended the operations.

Stuart himself was elated with the Confederate successes. He would write his cousin, "Our victories have been glorious beyond description," and he crowed of Robertson's efforts, "We knocked Buford's Brigade into Bull Run..." But, there was a dark cloud to the victory at Manassas. Staff member Captain James Hardeman Stuart, a cousin of the General, died while accompanying the 18th Mississippi in one of the last charges of the battle. He was the first member of Jeb's staff to die, but would not be the last.

ANTIETAM CAMPAIGN

On September 2, in fine fettle, Stuart reestablished his headquarters at Camp Qui Vive. He had much to cheer. The entire cavalry division had come together, and one of his more nettlesome subordinates, Beverly Robertson, had been replaced by Thomas Munford. On a broad front, Confederate hopes were soaring, with Lee looking to cap a summer of amazing victories. By September 5, the way seemed clear. After conferring with Lee, Longstreet, and Jackson, Stuart and his cavalry splashed across the Potomac and trotted into Maryland.

The army commander was planning to operate across the mountains from Frederick, and Stuart was to screen Lee's manuevers. Consequently, Jeb made his headquarters in Urbanna and fanned his troopers across a 20-mile arc covering all the roads leading to Washington. While the cavalry kept close watch on the Federal forces cloistered there, Jeb's staff commandeered the abandoned Urbanna Academy and organized a gala for the night of the 8th, "in honor of our arrival in Maryland." The ball had barely begun, however, when cannon fire announced a Federal thrust at one of the outposts. The officers rushed to the front, leaving the women in agonized suspense. Stuart and his staff returned at midnight with tales of Pelham's gallantry and their own high-spirited pursuit, but the arrival of the wounded turned the lady revellers into "ministering angels."

This would be but a brief respite for Stuart's boys, for serious pressure began to build against the cavalry screen. Slowly, his men fell back towards Frederick with Federal horse badgering them all the way. Amidst waving kerchiefs and bitter tears, Stuart departed Urbanna on the 11th, just minutes before the Bluecoats thundered into town. That night he managed a letter to Flora, noting that the "Ladies of Maryland make a great fuss over your husband," and boasting that "Marylanders are flocking by hundreds to our standards...". Actually, very few Marylanders joined Lee's army.

As the enemy pressed forward, Stuart's task was complicated by Lee's decision to divide his force by sending Jackson to seize Harper's Ferry while spreading Longstreet from Hagerstown to Boonsboro. Jackson in turn divided his divisions so as to advance upon the Ferry from three directions. With the army sprawled in so many directions, Stuart's men were put to the test of providing accurate and timely intelligence.

By the evening of the 12th, Jeb had picketed the gaps in the Catoctin range just west of Frederick. Although all seemed normal at first, events took an ominous turn the next afternoon. Stuart's men were pushed off the Catoctins and forced back to the craggy slopes of South Mountain. At dusk, from the heights of Turner's Gap, Stuart could see nothing but trouble—the valley between the Catoctins and South Mountain was dotted by hundreds of Federal campfires. Without doubt, McClellan was pursuing with uncharacteristic haste. In the emergency, Lee pushed D.H.Hill's troops into Turner's Gap and ordered Longstreet to come up in support. Stuart, meanwhile, sent Wade Hampton south to the Potomac to cover McLaws' Division and rushed Munford to bolster Confederate forces in Crampton's Gap, while placing Fitz Lee at Turner's. That night, he supplied General Roswell Ripley with a map of the area but before dawn was up and gone to check on Confederate affairs at Harper's Ferry.

Arriving on Maryland Heights, Stuart found the Federal garrison still holding out against Jackson's encircling forces. Even worse, to the north, the noise of battle reverberated. Stuart remained with McLaws for the day, but learned at dusk that the enemy had punched through Crampton's Gap. Riding ("as fast as our horses could carry us" as Von Borke recalled) to the sound of the guns, Stuart galloped into sheer chaos. Southern infantry, with Yankees in hot pursuit, were pouring out of the Gap into Pleasant Valley. Here Jeb rallied what fugitives he could and staunched the enemy advance. He then set a defensive line that secured the valley while guarding McLaws' rear. Further north, D.H. Hill had battled gamely with Longstreet's support but was eventually ordered off the mountain and south to Antietam Creek. Here Lee hoped to tarry long enough to allow Jackson to take the Ferry before rejoining the army. Clearly, the Maryland invasion was in shambles.

That night Stuart received intelligence that Lee's earlier orders outlining the campaign troop dispositions had fallen into Federal hands, which helped explain McClellan's aggressiveness. The following day, while his cavalry anchored the left of the Pleasant Valley line, Jackson's guns thundered at the Ferry. Suddenly, all went silent. Soon southern cheers filtered up from the Potomac along with word of the Federal surrender. Delighted at the news, Stuart threw his arms around 6'4"-250 pound Heros Von Borke and cried, "My dear Von, is this not glorious?" He then evacuated the Pleasant Valley line, sending a contingent to Lee near Sharpsburg while he and his staff rode south to join Jackson at the Federal surrender ceremonies. Afterwards, Jeb led Hampton and Munford's brigades north along the towpath of the Chesapeake and Ohio

Canal and on into Sharpsburg, arriving well after nightfall.

On the morning of September 16, Stuart gave General Lee a detailed brief of the Harper's Ferry surrender. When Jackson arrived around noon, Stuart fanned his cavalry to unmask McClellan's movements to the north. With Pelham's horse artillery "sweeping the field", Colonel Blackford soon uncovered the van of Federal infantry. That task complete, Stuart was next ordered to cover the army's left flank. This he did by occupying Nicodemus Heights and posting his horsemen on a line from the Potomac to Jackson's left flank. As night fell, the Federal presence was felt all around. Wrote Blackford: "It was quite clear...that the 17th would see a general engagement."

The following day, September 17, 1862, the Battle of Antietam raged from sunup to sundown. Fortunately for the Army of Northern Virginia— 38,000 strong—McClellan committed his 87,000 troops timidly and piecemeal, which enable Lee to stave off disaster by shifting units from one pressure point to another throughout the day. In the late afternoon, just when all seemed lost, the miraculous arrival of A. P. Hill's Light Division from Harper's Ferry saved Southern fortunes. The Union Ninth Corps was stopped in its tracks and the battle ended in stalemate—to the tune of 23,000 total casualties, making Antietam the bloodiest single day in American military history.

To Stuart's intense chagrin, his cavalry had played a minimal role. The terrain did not favor mounted assaults, and Pelham's artillery was the only element of his command that made a significant contribution. While Pelham pounded the right flank of various Yankee assault waves from his perch on Nicodemus Heights, Stuart and his staff roamed the field assisting where they could, with Jeb's horse being hit on one occasion. Only once was the cavalry asked to perform serious reconnaisance. Jackson requested intelligence on the Federal right flank near the Potomac, and Stuart was able to scout the position and warn against making an attack in an area swarming with Federals.

On September 18, the armies sat in place, licking their wounds. That evening, Lee ordered Stuart to examine the Potomac crossings in the army's rear. While Jeb's engineers pinpointed the river fords, Lee began his withdrawal. The crossing proved miserable. Rain turned the roads into a quagmire, and the fords were rocky and uneven. While in mid-river supervising the crossing, Stuart fell off his horse and escaped harm when Von Borke halted an oncoming wagon. Von Borke recalled that the General "was in great haste, and was calling out continually to those in front of him in somewhat angry tones." The teamsters answered in kind. Just before daylight, the exhausted cavalry finally came to rest south of the Potomac near Shepardstown and set up a rough camp, though their respite would be short-lived.

After a one-hour halt, Stuart was back in the saddle. To divert McClellan's pursuit, Lee ordered Jeb to take two of his cavalry brigades, his horse artillery, and two infantry regiments to threaten Williamsport, Maryland. Jeb marched immediately, and by noon, the Confederates had swept Williamsport clear of Yankees. Soon, Federal reinforcements arrived, and small arms fire and artillery erupted all along the line. Late that afternoon, some of Hampton's troopers fought their way to Hagerstown before enemy pressure forced their retreat. Although night-fall ended the fighting, some of the citizens of Williamsport invited Stuart and his staff to a party where "the time went merrily by..."

The next morning—September 20—Federal pressure built inexorably. Jeb remained well in front of his lines, examining the enemy positions with his usual energy. At one point, he and Von Borke barely avoided capture. Despite the enemy's preponderance, Stuart sensed an opportunity and ordered an incredulous Wade Hampton to advance on Hagerstown under the cover of darkness to operate in the Federal rear. But, as the sun set, Yankee artillery exploded in "a deafening cannonade," while Bluecoated infantry and cavalry pressed hard on the Confederate positions. Realizing that the game was up, Stuart recalled Hampton and, under the cover of Pelham's artillery, effected a night crossing of the Potomac. By midnight, Stuart and his troopers were in camp near Martinsburg. All were across, and the invasion of Maryland was over.

RIDING ANOTHER RAID

With Lee's battered army encamped around Winchester, Jeb established his headquarters at the Bower, the delightful plantation home of Stephen Dandridge, and began one of his more pleasant interludes of the war. "The open-hearted hospitality, the pleasant and ennobling social intercourse of those days, can never be forgotten," remembered adjutant H.B. McClellan. Even a Federal foray against Martinsburg—which an angry Stuart gave his brigadiers twenty minutes to suppress—couldn't dull the nightly excitement. Typical was the evening of October 7, when

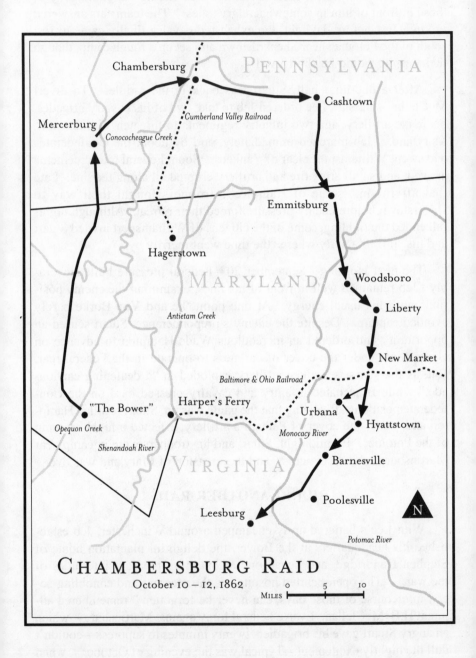

PENNSYLVANIA

Chambersburg

Cashtown

Mercerburg
Cumberland Valley Railroad

Conococheague Creek

Emmitsburg

Hagerstown

MARYLAND

Woodsboro

Antietam Creek

Liberty

New Market

Baltimore & Ohio Railroad

"The Bower"   Harper's Ferry

Urbana

Opequon Creek

Hyattstown

Monocacy River

Shenandoah River

VIRGINIA

Barnesville

Poolesville

N

Leesburg

Potomac River

Chambersburg Raid
October 10 – 12, 1862

MILES   0   5   10

the Bower hosted a ball for the local families. Amid the choruses of "Jine The Cavalry" and "Lorena" that lasted until dawn, the massive Von Borke recreated the part of a Pennsylvania farmer's wife in a pantomine that had the assembled roaring with laughter. Jeb was moved to announce, "My dear old Von...your appearance as a woman would never fade from my memory."

. The next day Von Borke delivered a present from General Stuart to Stonewall Jackson, a "stunning" uniform coat that Jeb had ordered from Richmond. After expressing his appreciation, Jackson attempted to put the gift away, but Von Borke wheedled Stonewall into donning the coat. Before long, stunned members of Jackson's command came running to headquarters to see their leader in his new appointments. Stonewall would send a note of thanks to Jeb, signing it, "Your much attached friend."

War again intervened. Lee desired Stuart to cut the railroad at Chambersburg, Pennsylvania and gather intelligence on Federal positions and intentions; he also wanted to Stuart to take civilian hostages to exchange for Virginians seized during Pope's recent campaign. Here was a mission after Jeb's own heart—another chance to ride around the Federals. As staff member Channing Price put it, "General Stuart's long suppressed desire to pay a visit to Pennsylvania & especially Chambersburg (would be) gratified."

Elements from all three of Stuart's brigades were included in the expedition. Rooney Lee replaced an ailing Fitz Lee, and, as usual, Pelham brought four of his guns. In a heavy fog near sunrise on the 10th, the column lunged into Maryland. At 8:00 am they crossed the National Pike west of Hagerstown, and by 10:00 am, were trotting into Pennsylvania. Stuart paused to hear his simple orders read to each command: horses would be impressed, and private property would be respected. But one command rang above all others: "(B)ehave with no other thought than victory." Cheers greeted Jeb's exhortation, the troopers "wild with enthusiasm."

As storm clouds gathered, the men swarmed across the countryside gathering up horses. Despite orders against pillaging, Charles Blackford observed many a Pennsylvania "pantry" inspection. A shocked civilian populace watched as their horses were confiscated in droves. On the raiders swept, north through Mercersburg then east towards the Cumberland Valley Railroad. By now northern telegraph lines were buzzing, but few if any Yankees showed themselves. At dark, forty miles from their starting point, Stuart and his staff gathered on a hill just west of Chambersburg. Pelham arranged his guns while Wade Hampton entered the town with a demand for surrender. The parley proved brief. Before long, Stuart had Chambersburg locked down.

Since the city fathers had fled with the bank's holdings, the town coffers were empty. What was worse, the main objective of the raid, the Cumberland Valley Railroad bridge, was of iron construction, and the Confederate wrecking crew couldn't dent it. Meanwhile, threatening clouds gave way to a drenching rainstorm, turning the roadways to mud and the rivers to torrents. Stuart himself had reached another crossroads. Another ride around McClellan was "fixed in his mind," but an unfordable Potomac River could prove disasterous.

At dawn, while a detachment remained in Chambersburg to destroy the military stores, the weary column slogged east towards Gettysburg. At the head of the line, Jeb called Charles Blackford to his side to explain his reasons for adopting this route of return. The hilly country to the west would be easily defended by the pursuing enemy, but the open country to the east allowed greater flexibility of movement. Plus, the Potomac fords downriver would be harder for the Yankees to defend and, thus, easier to rush successfully. Above all, Stuart knew his enemy; they simply wouldn't believe the Confederates might hazard another such circling of their army. Blackford assured the General that he concurred completely and that he would publicize his General's motives should Jeb fall.

In order to ensure silence, orders were given forbidding the use of firearms. Luckily, the horses couldn't raise dust on the wet roads. Up and over the craggy slopes of South Mountain wound the command, then south along its eastern base. Around sundown, the troopers entered the town of Emmitsburg to the cheers of the pro-Southern populace. Nodding their appreciation, Stuart's grim faced troopers passed through and on into the night. Riders swayed in their saddles and suffered sleep-starved hallucinations while "snores could be heard above other sounds." The rebels could do little but endure their "long, terrible night."

The column passed to the east of Frederick through Woodsboro to New Market. After crossing the B&O Railroad, Stuart approached Charles Blackford and asked if he would like to visit the New York Rebel at their old Urbanna headquarters, the Cockey home. The engineer needed little prodding. He joined other staff members on their sojourn, but their "delighful" visit was necessarily short. Blackford always assumed Stuart made the sidetrip to see what the Cockey's knew of Federal postings in the area, but, whether chivalry or professional considerations prompted the detour, Stuart soon ordered his staff back to the main column. At daylight on October 12, the wayward party rejoined their comrades near Hyattstown, with the Potomac but twelve miles away.

By now Jeb knew that the Yankees controlled both the mouth of the Monocacy to the west and the fords near Leesburg. Entering Barnesville, he learned too that Union cavalry had just cleared the area, another bad sign. With his options narrowed, Stuart turned to Benjamin White, and the Marylander didn't disappoint. Stuart purposely allowed the column to be seen by Federal signallers on Sugar Loaf Mountain, after which White led the column onto an old farm road that entered the road to the Potomac west of town. Up ahead, a Federal squadron rode toward the van of the column, lulled into complacency by the fact that many Rebels were wearing confiscated blue overcoats. When Stuart ordered a charge, the startled Yanks responded with a hurried volley then scattered, leaving the road to White's Ford wide open.

Rooney Lee arrived at the Potomac first where he found Federal infantry lining a quarry just south of the ford. Borrowing an earlier Stuart tactic, Lee decided to bluff them by sending a demand of surrender assuring the Yankees of annhilation if they didn't comply in fifteen minutes. To his amazement, the Bluecoats began withdrawing, and the Confederates were soon splashing across unopposed into Virginia. Pelham's guns cooled enemy pressure on the flanks, but the rearguard had lost contact with the column. Determined not to lose any part of his command so close to home, Stuart dispatched Charles Blackford to bring them in at the gallop. Minutes later, the "lost" rear guard came pounding down a corridor held open by the "gallant" Pelham and his guns. With Yankees swarming against the Maryland bank of the river, the last of Stuart's raiders galloped through the shoals of White's Ford and into Virginia.

Later critics would harp that Stuart's Chambersburg raid was a pointless, risky venture of little worth to the Confederate cause. The fact that it was ordered by Lee seemed to make little difference to those hindsighted few. However, the facts are simple. All told, the raiders covered 126 miles, the final 80 in thirty-six hours. With the loss of sixty mounts and no troopers, the column confiscated 1200 badly needed horses and caused upwards of $250,000 worth of damage to Northern military property. It made McClellan and his cavalry again look foolish and raised the prestige of the Southern horsemen to even greater heights. As to its riskiness, Charles Blackford noted simply, "(T)he opposition of their cavalry was considered of very little account by us." As a matter of course, the press extolled the heroism of the Confederate cavalry. Most importantly, Robert E. Lee judged the enterprise "eminently successful," even with the rail bridge at Chambersburg still standing. Not surprisingly, Jeb himself thought the expedition a "brilliant success...without parallel in history." To his mind," the hand of God was clearly manifested."

GATHERING CLOUDS

On October 13, Jeb and his band returned in glee to the Dandridge family headquarters "The 'Bower' is a charming place, full of pretty girls," wrote Stuart to a female cousin, but the General had professional obligations as well. First, on October 16, just as a celebratory ball had ended, Stuart was called out to assist Jackson in shooing a division of McClellan's infantry back across the Potomac. Then on the 24th, Jeb requested that Colonel Thomas Munford be made a brigadier assigned to Robertson's former command. Of Robertson's intended replacement, Grumble Jones, Stuart was adamant: "I do not regard Brigadier General Jones...as a fit person to command a brigade of Cavalry...if there are any who entertain different views in regard to General Jones, let such have the benefit of his services and talents." Furthermore, Stuart recommended that a fourth brigade be formed with Colonel Thomas Rosser in command, and in light of the "conspicuous gallantry, ability and efficiency of Major John Pelham in action," Jeb desired his artillery officer be made a Lieutenant Colonel. The General had some firm ideas of who should lead his brigades, and he used firm language—"profoundly impressed with the correctness of my views"—to make his point.

Two days later, McClellan brushed aside Confederate cavalry pickets and threw two divisions over the Potomac east of Harper's Ferry. Lee countered by moving Longstreet's divisions south and ordered Stuart to protect Longstreet's advance. In the pouring rain of October 29, Jeb bade regretful adieu to the Bower. Sometime the next day, Stuart climbed the heights of Snicker's Gap, where he observed the advance of the Army of the Potomac.

Stuart's assignment gave him three Blue Ridge gaps to defend—from the north: Snicker's, Ashby's, and Manassas—and a line to hold from Front Royal to Longstreet's destination at Culpeper. Despite a high incidence of sick horses and dismounted riders, he refused to settle for a static defense of his perimeter. Leaving Grumble Jones with Jackson, Stuart himself took Fitz Lee's brigade (now commanded by Colonel John Wickham) and went hunting for Yankees. At sunrise of the 31st, the Gray troopers thundered down on the Federal outpost near Mountsville and chased them east through Aldie over the Bull Run Mountains. As they cleared the gap, the Confederates could see the country from Leesburg to Centreville "crawling with the blue army." Jeb pulled his boys after encountering Federal cavalry, realizing that Federal cavalry commander Alfred Pleasanton couldn't be far behind.

Pleasanton arrived, all right, pounding down on the outnumbered Rebels with a determined fury. For two days, "endless" fighting flared first near the small towns of Bloomfield and Union, then around Upperville and Middleburg. Somehow, the Confederate horse bitterly hung on to the area east of Snicker's Gap, with Pelham's guns blasting holes and emptying many a Federal saddle. When Blackford discovered that McClellan's entire army was moving south just behind the Federal cavalry screen, Stuart ordered Hampton up to protect the passes, freeing Jeb and Fitz Lee's brigade to probe the Federal advance. On the morning of the 4th, Hampton defeated an enemy force near the hamlet of Markham. But, the hardest fighting of the week erupted the next day near Barbee's Crossroads, as Hampton and Stuart slammed into Federal horsemen southeast of Manassas Gap. Losses mounted as the two forces—fighting both mounted and dismounted—viciously clashed. Only once did the Federals manage to penetrate Stuart's left and catch a glimpse of Confederate infantry marching south. It was, in all, a masterful job performance by rebel cavalry.

Unfortunately, Stuart now began receiving bitter news from home. Little Flora had become ill in late October, and a string of messages advised the General of her worsening condition. Finally, during the night of the 5th, the heartbreaking word arrived: Flora Stuart had died on November 3rd. Von Borke saw the dispatch first and went to wake the General. When Jeb roused, he saw the look of concern on the Prussian's face and asked if the Yankees were advancing. Von Borke simply handed him the missive and stood there as Stuart read the note. "(H)e threw his arms around my neck, and wept bitter tears...," was Von Borke's recollection, adding that "My dear General never recovered from this cruel blow."

On the 6th, Stuart led a squad north of the Rapidan and found the enemy. The Bluecoats reponded vigorously, and fighting raged for the remainder of the day. That night, a severe early winter snowstorm blanketed the area. The hard service had worn down Southern mounts to a dangerous degree, so that when the Federal horse came on mid-morning, Stuart had to order two artillery pieces buried for lack of transportation. His troopers fought a day-long delaying action to the Hazel River which, in a blowing snowstorm, they forded late that night.

With Lee's army concentrated at Culpeper for what appeared to be an extended stay, Jeb wired Flora to visit him. In the meantime, he had begun to show some frustration with his troopers' performance. During an encounter on the 10th, Fitz Lee's boys were roughly handled by a Federal advance. A seething Stuart deliberately drew enemy fire, and when his staff warned him of the danger of his position, he sneeringly invited them to leave at their liberty. Just then, in a hail of musketry, the General rubbed his face. The staff discovered that half of Jeb's moustache had been pared clean by a Yankee slug. Said Von Borke, "I could not help laughing heartily..."

On November 11, Flora arrived and many officers, Robert E. Lee included, offered their heart-felt sympathy over little Flora's death. Jeb's concern for his wife at this point was apparent—"(she) is not herself since the loss of her little companion"—but the blow upon the General was telling also—"I can think over her sweet little face, sweet temper and nature and extraordinary susceptibilities and weep like a child...". To Flora, Jeb would fatalistically confide, "I feel perfect resignation to go at (God's) bidding, and join my little Flora."

FREDERICKSBURG

In early November, George McClellan was replaced as Army of the Potomac commander by Ambrose Burnside. When, in December, Burnside sidled his army east toward Fredricksburg, Lee ordered a quick concentration of his forces along the hills west of the town. From his headquarters—"Camp No Camp"—five miles south on the Telegraph Road, Stuart directed his brigades in covering a fifty-mile front along the Rappahannock. Outwardly, "Camp No Camp" retained a festive appearance. There was this season, however, an underlying gloom prompted not only by little Flora's death but the loss of Redmond Burke, one of Stuart's favorite scouts.

At dawn on December 11, Lee, Longstreet, and Stuart gathered on some high ground to watch the Federal artillery pound Fredricksburg to rubble. By day's end, Union troops had bridged the river and swarmed into the gutted streets of the once beautiful city. With the left of Lee's infantry safely anchored on the Rappahannock, Jeb concentrated his troopers on Lee's right and awaited the Federal assault.

He spent much of the 12th scouting the developing Union assault base. Finally, in the thick fog of the following morning, the ponderous Federal army moved forward. Among the waiting Confederates, flags waved and a band blared martial music. Just then, Stonewall Jackson appeared before his men resplendent in his new uniform, courtesy of the cavalry commander. When teased by his staff, Jackson replied, "It's the doing of my friend Stuart, I believe."

As the Federal artillery opened, Stuart galloped to John Pelham and his horse artilley in advance of Jackson's right flank. When the fog lifted to reveal the massive Blue-clad battle lines in assault array, Stuart sent Lee a final posting: "I am going to crowd them with artillery." He then ordered Pelham to engage the Federals with his two guns, though one piece was disabled almost immediately. Continuing the duel with his remaining gun, the "Boy Cannoneer" ripped at the flank of the advancing Union infantry lines with telling effect. When four Federal batteries opened on the single Confederate cannon, Stuart ordered him out of the barrage, but Pelham withdrew only after his ammunition finally gave out. Observed General Lee of Pelham's actions, "It is glorious to see such courage in one so young."

The Federals bled themselves dry assaulting Lee's positions west of Fredricksburg. In only one sector, a marshy gap in A. P. Hill's line, did the Yankees make a breakthrough of sorts, but the breach was sealed quickly. As at Antietam, Jeb spent most of the day chafing for opportunities that never developed while the opposing infantrymen slugged it out. By nightfall, the carnage had ended and Jeb could write Flora, "I got shot through my fur collar but am unhurt." Unfortunately for the South, the Fredricksburg bloodletting was of no strategic importance. Earlier Jackson had predicted a barren victory, and the prediction was true enough.

As the Union troops settled in north of the Rappahannock, Lee's men transformed the area west of Fredricksburg into a vast winter bivouac. Stuart's staff quickly outfitted "Camp No Camp" to the tastes of their commander. Jackson was nearby, having established his headquarters in the office outbuilding on the Corbin Plantation. Sporting appointments—a reflection of the gaming tastes of the owner—adorned Stonewall's headquarters. At Christmas dinner, Jeb playfully derided the trappings of "blood sports" as an indication of low breeding, and claimed that a pat of butter stamped with a gamecock was a sure sign of "moral degeneracy" even as he intoned that it was Jackson's coat-of-arms. Lee also joined in the ribbing when he claimed that Stonewall and his staff, ensconced as they were in such commodious luxury, were merely "playing soldiers." Amidst the laughter, Jackson merely smiled tightly and blushed "like a girl."

As the New Years approached, General Lee ordered a large scale operation against Federal communications. In a veil of secrecy, Jeb assembled 600 troopers from each of his three brigades along with Pelham and four of his guns, and put the column on the road the day after Christmas. Crossing the Rappahannock at Kelly's Ford, they camped for the evening near Bristerburg just south of Cedar Run. On the following morning, Stuart swung into action.

Fitz Lee was detailed to sever the Telegraph Road at Chopowamsic and then head north, while Rooney Lee hit the town of Dumfries from the west. Wade Hampton meanwhile was to take the town of Occoquan to the north and then to rendezvous with the two Lee's at Dumfries. However, when Rooney and Fitz joined up near Dumfries, Stuart found a brigade of enemy infantry defending the place. After a few hours of ineffectual manuever, the Confederates disengaged and trotted north towards Occoquan where they found Wade Hampton near Cole's Store. After an evening of rest, Stuart sent his captures south along with two of Pelham's guns, and then directed his entire force back towards Occoquan. At Greenwood Church, Fitz Lee routed two regiments of Union cavalry and pursued them all the way to their camps in town. As the Federals dispersed, gray troopers whirled through Occoquan and began a spree of destruction that lasted until dark. Jeb then reordered his force and headed north into the winter night.

The column reached the Orange and Alexandria Railroad at Burke's Station just a few miles west of Alexandria. While the troopers tore up the tracks in both directions, Jeb took possession of the local telegraph office and monitored the fevered Federal communications. After a few hours of tracking enemy reponse to the raid, Jeb the prankster could contain himself no longer. He telegrammed a message of complaint to Union authorities in Washington that the poor muleflesh he was encountering "interfered seriously with our moving the captured wagons." With that, he severed the wire and moved to later roust the alarmed Yankee garrison near Fairfax Courthouse. By the 29th, the raiders halted west of Vienna before moving on to Culpeper on the last day of the year.

With the timing of a great actor, Jeb Stuart and his cavalry triumphantly returned to their camps south of Fredricksburg on New Year's Day. With some justification, Channing Price called it the cavalry's "longest, most dangerous and most brilliant expedition" of the war. Some three hundred prisoners, two hundred horses, twenty wagonloads of Yankee supplies and equipment, and "a trail of confusion and embarassment" marked the Dumfries Raid. The loss to the Confederates was minimal: one killed, thirteen wounded, and thirteen missing. The press may not have labeled it as such, but Jeb Stuart had once again ridden a raid around the humiliated Federals.

1863

January and February passed with little excitement for Stuart and his troopers. Rain and snow turned Northern Virginia into a vast mud field, thus restricting mobility. The cavalry continued to picket the Rappahannock and clashed occasionally with Federal reconnaissance patrols, but the largest action of the period was a two-day snowball fight among the various infantry brigades. Only once, near the end of February, did the Confederates mount an expedition, with Fitz Lee thrusting at the Federal rear and capturing 155 men and horses.

Flora visited headquarters at this time and by mid-February was expecting another child. Indeed, Jeb Stuart seemed his old self, "going out frolicking" and "rous(ing) up the whole camp by his singing and shouting." Still, there was much cavalry business to attend to. He pushed for the official advancement of a number of his officers, in particular Thomas Rosser and John Pelham, and continued to beg for Grumble Jones' removal. Stuart also crossed swords with Wade Hampton, prompting the South Carolinian to complain, "All my time and correspondence of late have been taken up in quarelling with Stuart." Nor was Hampton alone: staffer Thomas Price also found Stuart somewhat tiresome, complaining that the General "prattled on all evening in his garrulous way." In an army loaded with fractious personalities, the flamboyant Stuart was a lightening rod for criticism.

On March17th, while Stuart was staying in Culpeper, intelligence arrived that the Federals had forced the nearby Kelly's Ford. Fitz Lee commanded the local Confederate defenses, and he had managed to blunt the Federal advance—some 2100 troopers—with his 800 horsemen. Arriving on the scene with artilleryman Pelham, Stuart let Lee fight the fight, but Jeb couldn't contain himself as he rallied a stalled movement with the cry, "Confound it men, come back! Don't leave me alone here." Naturally, Pelham helped spur the artillery on, but as Harry Gilmor and the "Boy Cannoneer" were observing part of the clash, some Federal artilley got their range. After a particularly close shellburst, Gilmor found Pelham lying on the ground. The boy's face was wide-eyed and calm, but blood poured from a wound in the back of his skull. Gilmor dismounted and wrestled the limp body onto his horse, then ordered two cavalrymen to bring the wounded artillerist back to Culpeper. When he located his commander and told him the news, an incredulous Jeb Stuart "bowed on his horse's neck and wept."

Later that night, without regaining consciousness, the "gallant" John Pelham passed away. At the Shackleford House in Culpeper, the weeping Stuart bade farewell by snipping a lock of his gunner's hair and tenderly kissing his forehead. Following so quickly on little Flora's passing, Pelham's death was devastating and Stuart composed effusive tributes to the young man's memory. But it was to Flora that he revealed a deepening fatalism: "You must know how (Pelham's) death distressed me...I shall religiously observe your wishes..in case I survive you, which is so extremely improbable..."

Jeb arrived in Richmond the day after Pelham's funeral, "greatly grieved" that he had missed the ceremonies, but there was more than Pelham's death disturbing the cavalryman. Since the Chambersburg Raid, Jeb had lost his little Flora, Redmond Burke, and now, John Pelham. Additionally, the Confederate cavalry had been roughly handled in the Loudon Valley. The Dumfries Raid restored some of their lost luster, but when the officers reconvened at Camp No Camp, Von Borke noted a change in the atmosphere: "All these misfortunes did not fail to cast a gloom over our little military family." Little did they know that their greatest trial was about to begin.

PEAKING

By April, new Federal Commander Joseph Hooker had organized his cavalry into one, powerful 13,000 man corps. Concurrently, Stuart was begging Lee to concentrate his own cavalry. With Grumble Jones' brigade west of the Blue Ridge and Hampton's resting and refitting,

Jeb had a mere 2000 troopers at his disposal. But Robert E. Lee sent Jones to West Virginia and ordered Jeb to use his "good management, boldness, and discretion" to offset the nearly 6 to 1 Yankee superiority. Early on the morning of April 28, Stuart was put to the test. Federal infantry began spilling over Kelly's Ford and lunging at the Rapidan crossings, while Union cavalry crossed Kelly's the next day and headed west. Ordered to protect public property near Gordonsville, Stuart sent Rooney Lee with two regiments to shadow the Federal horse, leaving Fitz Lee's brigade to harass the Federal infantry advance and collect as much intelligence as possible.

The opening phase of the battle of Chancellorsville was Jeb Stuart at his finest. Gray cavalry sent Lee precise reports pinpointing Federal movements and troop dispositions. Telegraphic communication proved defective, but Lee in Fredricksburg soon knew that three Federal corps were in the process of circling his left flank. Meanwhile, Rebel horsemen were everywhere, aggressively snapping at the enemy, teaching the Federals that the area's roadways "were likely to be dominated by Jeb Stuart's cavalry."

Stuart joined Lee on the morning of May 1. As the Commanding General—outnumbered almost 2 to 1—boldly pushed his army westward towards the tangled forests of the Wilderness to confront the Yankees, Stuart's cavalry provided a moving screen, with Jeb accompanying Jackson's men on the Rebel left. As the two armies came to grips in the heavy woods, Jeb spent the day probing the Union lines until they located what they believed to be the Federal flank anchored near an iron furnace. Stuart opened with his horse artillery, now commanded by Major Robert Beckham, and was shelled heavily in return. One shell exploded near Jeb's staff, and a small fragment struck his gifted aide-de-camp Channing Price in the leg, severing an artery. By midnight Price was gone, another valued member of Stuart's staff dead on the field.

That night, Jackson and Lee resolved to try a sneak attack against the unsupported Yankee right flank. On May 2, while Lee held the front, Fitz Lee's troopers led a day-long march of Jackson's three divisions slipping around the Federal rear. Near six pm, Jeb watched Jackson's men come whooping oout the woods to begin rolling up the Federal Eleventh Corps. Determined to maximize his victory, Jackson continued his assault into the night. Stuart meanwhile moved north to seal off Ely's Ford on the Rappahannock, but a member of A.P. Hill's staff arrived with devastating news: both Hill and Jackson were knocked out of action, with Stonewall badly wounded. Moreover, Jackson had ordered Stuart to assume command of his corps, which made up over half the Confederate army at Chancellorsville.

It was a situation unprecedented in the American Civil War. Never before and never again would a cavalry officer take command of so large an infantry force under such duress. Since Jackson's staff had departed with their wounded chief and his own staff was up near Ely's Ford, Jeb was forced to improvise on his own. At midnight, after sending word of the development to Robert E. Lee, he spent the rest of the night shoring up and aligning the ragged Confederate battle line. "It is necessary that the glorious victory thus far achieved be prosecuted with the utmost vigor" he told Lee. Through the ordeal, Stuart's prodigious energy served him well.

Shortly before dawn, artillery commander E. P. Alexander reported that a piece of open high ground occupied by the Federals—Hazel Grove to the locals—commanded their position. Stuart immediately determined to seize it. As the sun rose, his men moved forward. Soon the entire line was ablaze with musketry. Resplendent in a new blue broadcloth uniform, Stuart seemed everywhere, pressing the infantry against the teetering Federal defenses, even leaping his horse over some crude breastworks in an effort to drive the attacks home. At one point he bluffed a Union battleline into inaction by issuing bold commands to cease firing. At another he advanced several batteries under stinging fire, prompting one witness to describe it as "the bravest act I ever saw."

Shouting orders (when he wasn't singing "Old Joe Hooker, come out of the Wilderness") Jeb personally led his infantry up the bloody, tangled ridge to Hazel Grove until the Yankee line snapped under the pressure. Alexander quickly pulled his guns onto the heights and turned the Chancellorsville clearing into an inferno. By 10:30 am, it was all over. A beaten Joe Hooker eventually pulled his troops north towards the Rappahannock while Stuart and Lee united their forces in victory. Complaints of the casualties suffered under Stuart on May 2 surfaced later, but E. P. Alexander said it all when he wrote, "I do not think there was a more brilliant thing done in the war than Stuart's extricating that command..."

The price of victory was high, for Chancellorsville had cost the the life of the irreplaceable Stonewall Jackson. When it was reported that

Jackson made a deathbed request that Jeb take over his corps, Stuart was said to reply, "I would rather know that Jackson said that than to have the appointment." Forced to regroup, Lee now reorganized his army into three separate corps commanded in numerical sequence by James Longstreet, Richard Ewell, and A.P. Hill. Realizing that something needed to be done to offset the huge Federal numerical advantage in cavalry, Lee finally acceded to Stuart's wishes and ordered a concentration of all available horsemen. As a consequence, Jeb Stuart now found himself in command of nearly 10,000 troopers.

On May 22, he reviewed three of his brigades near Culpeper. Encouraged by the martial display and obviously sensing a need to build espirit in his new command, Jeb ordered a grand review of his entire force at Brandy Station. Invitations were issued and word of the review spread quickly. On June 4, Culpeper became the social center of Virginia as trainloads of visitors arrived to view the next day's spectacle. And, spectacle it was. June 5 saw Stuart at the peak of his glory as he watched a one a half mile-long line of grayclad troopers thrill a mass of viewers with charges and counter-charges. The men cheered and the ladies swooned, prompting one jaded artillerist to admit, "it was one of the grandest scenes I ever saw." Wrote Heros Von Borke, "We all looked with pride upon this magnificient body of troops." That night, bonfires lit an open air ball near cavalry headquarters, with Stuart playing the proud host.

Only one thing could have improved the June 5 festivities: the presence of Robert E. Lee. Caught up in organizing his army for an invasion of Maryland and Pennsylvania, Lee had been busy elsewhere. As his columns began converging on Culpeper, however, Marse Robert sent word that he could review the cavalry on the 8th. Many of Stuart's men grumbled, perhaps unaware that the Commanding General himself had requested the second review. Nevertheless, on the appointed day, the cavalry repeated its evolutions for their commander, with similiar precision but less fanfare. Having been asked to "bring his people," John Bell Hood mischieviously brought not his staff but his whole division. Catcalls between the troopers and the infantrymen were exchanged, good-naturedly and otherwise, but Lee was impressed, writing his wife, "It was a splendid sight...Stuart was in all his glory."

That night Jeb retired to a simple camp on nearby Fleetwood Hill. Pickets settled in along the Rappahannock fords as the cavalrymen bedded down for their final night on the plains of Brandy Station. At 4:30

am, June 9, 1863, two strike forces of Federal cavalry and infantry—10,000 men in all—came boiling over the Rappahannock River.

PLAINS OF BRANDY

Jolted awake by the explosion of battle roiling down from the north, Stuart immediately ordered both Fitz Lee and Wade Hampton to march toward the sound of the guns. When word came that the enemy had also forced Kelly's Ford, Jeb threw 1st South Carolina into the breach pending the arrival of Beverly Robertson's brigade. Leaving the 2nd South Carolina to protect Fleetwood Heights and sending the headquarters baggage to Culpeper, Stuart rode north.

Hampton's men were the first on the scene. There they found Grumble Jones' boys and Beckham's artillery holding off a large Federal force near St. James Church. Rooney Lee came up and positioned his brigade along Yew Ridge, extending Jones' line to the north. Despite the small Union success, Grumble Jones had fought the Bluecoats to a stalemate, and when Jeb arrived, he found the Federal advance "apparently abandoned." But, just before noon Jones's scouts reported that an enemy force was advancing on Brandy Station from the south. On the assumption that Robertson's troopers could handle that threat, Stuart directed Jones to look to his front while he himself protected the flank. Unaware of Jeb's dispositions, Grumble lived up to his nickname. In a profane explosion, he announced, "So he thinks they ain't coming, does he? Well, let him alone; he'll damned soon see for himself."

As Jeb watched the two lines slug it out, word came from staffer Major Henry McClellan that the enemy were advancing in force on the Fleetwood Heights. Jeb was incredulous: Robertson's force should have prevented just such a movement. However, when artillery reports echoed up from the south, Stuart reacted quickly, pulling two of Jones' regiments and two of Beckham's guns out of line to send them to the direction of the fighting. Wade Hampton too heard the firing and broke off his fight to counter the threat to his rear. In the wink of an eye, Brandy Station was up for grabs as thousands of horsemen Blue and Gray converged on Fleetwood Hill.

Staffer Henry McClellan had fought a courageous, if lonely, holding action by deploying one six-pound howitzer on the crest of the hill. When his ammunition was gone, McClellan helplessly watched as the Federal cavalry rode to within 50 yards of his position. However, as the Federals crested the ridge, Jones' units began arriving. Thus began a series of rapid charges and countercharges that characterized the fight at Brandy. Jones' units broke against the massed Federals, but hard-charging Confederate reinforcements swept most of the enemy off the heights. The Southerners took special note of Union artillery positioned along the southwest slope of Fleetwood—only six of these Union artillerists survived the battle but their reinforcements saved the guns from capture. The 1st South Carolina and Cobb's Legion cleared the hill of the remaining enemy, but just as Hampton's troopers arrived, a three-regiment Federal cavalry assault swept up the Heights from the open ground east near the railroad.

Hampton's boys slammed two of the Yankee regiments into pieces, but the third enemy unit swung into the Confederate rear and made off with a battle flag and a number of prisoners before passing completely over the hill and escaping to the west. Meanwhile, Beckham arrived with his artillery to consolidate the rebel hold on Fleetwood, while Hampton raced across the plain to the east towards the railroad in pursuit of the disorganized Unionists. A lethargic Federal attempt to flank the hill from the direction of Stevensburg came to naught, and slowly, the bitter fighting around Fleetwood Hill flickered out.

Back to the north, the Federals had pried Rooney Lee off of Yew Ridge, but the Confederates simply retreated to an equally strong position on the northern extension of Fleetwood. Around 3:30 pm, fighting on that front was reignited but proved indecisive. Eventually, the enemy backed off. Soon, the Northerners were pulling back all along the front and recrossing the Rappahannock, and the Battle of Brandy Station— the largest cavalry action in American history—came to an end.

Jeb would write Flora that the battle "was no surprise." Obviously, he refused to accept the truth. The Federal crossings of the Rappahannock caught Stuart's cavalry totally unaware, but Grumble Jones had risen to the occasion and, in a large part, been responsible for cancelling the enemy's advantage. Rooney Lee's men also deserved accolades for fighting John Buford's tough Yankees to a standstill. But, Stuart was ill-served by the incompetent Beverly Robertson who failed utterly in hindering the Federal movement across Kelly's Ford. In the clashes north of Brandy Station, Wade Hampton stood out, stoutly defending the Heights and aggressively chasing the Blueclad horsemen beyond the railroad. And, in the center of it all rode Jeb Stuart. Exercising superb battlefield command, he "eked out the narrowest of tactical victories" in the most trying of conditions. Stuart drew much criticism for Brandy Station—some justified, some not—but, in the end, the Federals had been checked and still had no idea where Lee's infantry was, thanks to Jeb and his cavalry.

EYES NORTH

As the Army of Northern Virginia moved north down the Shenandoah Valley, Lee ordered Stuart east of the Blue Ridge to screen the advance. Accordingly, on June 16 the cavalry splashed across the Rappahannock and occupied the Loudon Valley. With his headquarters in Middleburg, Stuart directed Fitz Lee's brigade—commanded now by Thomas Munford—to Aldie, and Rooney Lee's brigade—commanded by J.R. Chambliss—to Thoroughfare Gap. On the 17th, as Munford occupied Aldie, Federal cavalry stormed into the village and initiated a day-long fight. Neither side gained an advantage and Munford eventually broke off the encounter, but Stuart and his staff barely escaped capture when a lone Federal cavalry regiment burst into Middleburg from the south. Stuart quickly struck back by ordering in Robertson, who soon pushed the Yanks south of town, where they were virtually destroyed the next morning by Chambliss' men.

On that same morning of the 17th, powerful Federal cavalry columns pushed west from Aldie, but Munford stymied them east of Snicker's Gap and Stuart blunted another enemy force just west of Middleburg. By evening, both Federal columns had retreated back to Aldie, but the morning of the 19th found the Northerners again pressing Stuart near Middleburg. This time things did not go well for the Southerners. Robertson's men broke under a dismounted assault, and, as the Confederate lines stiffened, Heros Von Borke was seriously wounded in the neck. To the north, however, Jones held off a thrust by John Buford's men and Chambliss prevented a flanking force from effecting a juncture with the main enemy column. Once again, Stuart had foiled the Yankee attempts to penetrate the Rebel screen.

Captured dispatches confirmed the obvious, that the mission of the Yankee cavalry was to pinpoint the whereabouts of Lee's infantry. Stuart therefore redeployed his brigades to plug the gaps in the Blue Ridge. Wade Hampton reinforced Robertson's forces covering Ashby Gap while Chambliss and Grumble Jones protected the town of Union. Meanwhile, Munford remained at Snickersville. After a rainy 20th of June allowed Stuart to consolidate his positions, the Federal cavalry reappeared on the 21st, this time backed up by infantry. Hampton held off the repeated thrusts as long as he could, but one enemy rush disabled an artillery piece and Stuart's horse artillery lost its first cannon ever to the Federals.

With the appearance of enemy infantry, Stuart knew the game was up, but he fought a masterful series of delaying actions all the way to the foot of the Blue Ridge near Upperville. To the north, Jones and Chambliss also employed a fighting withdrawal and succeeded in uniting with Stuart at Upperville. Jones' men fought especially well as they sealed the rift caused by another of Robertson's breakdowns, and, by nightfall, Stuart and his reunited command joined Lafayette McLaw's supporting division in the hills west of Upperville. The Federals may have been flushed with a sense of victory, but when they withdrew to Aldie the next day, followed closely by Confederate videttes, they still had no idea as to the whereabouts of Lee's infantry.

To those watching, Stuart's command style had altered dramatically during the Loudon Valley encounters. Henry McClellan watched him delegate authority to his subordinates to the point of becoming little more than a bystander to the fighting. A perplexed McClellan asked his commander why he had adopted this tack. Stuart reponded that "he wished them to feel the responsibility resting upon them and gain whatever honor the field might bring." Later commentators see this as evidence of Stuart of losing faith in himself, but the truth is much simpler. With the mounting losses among his officer corps and staff (at the time, Von Borke's wound appeared mortal) and his own fatalistic leanings, Jeb Stuart was more likely preparing his troops for the day when he too would be gone.

TO RIDE AGAIN

On June 22, Stuart had received first orders from General Lee concerning his cavalry's role in the grand invasion. Lee's directive was rather simple: if Stuart found the Yankees moving northward, he was to cross the Potomac with three brigades and connect with the army's advance somewhere near the Susquehanna River. James Longstreet was privy to these orders and warned Jeb not to disclose the army's intentions by "passing to our rear," twice commenting on Stuart's "proposed route in rear of the enemy." Late the next day, Lee again communicated with Jeb about the operation. This second set of orders was burdened by fair amount of imprecision but seemed to insist that Stuart cross the Potomac at Shepardstown if the Union army "not appear to be moving northward." Lee also requested that his remaining two brigades protect the Blue Ridge passes and close up on the Confederate rear should Stuart "cross the river east of the mountains." If the Yankees were shadowing the Confederate invasion, Lee evidently wanted his cavalry operating in their rear.

Twenty years after the war, Henry McClellan recalled a third message from Lee on June 23. In this one, Lee expressed the fear that the delay in the infantry's Potomac crossings west of the Blue Ridge made it necessary for Stuart to cross the river east of the mountains and to pass in the enemy rear. Lee left the matter to Stuart's discretion but suggested that if he should pass in the enemy rear he should look for General Jubal Early's division near York, Pennsylvania, the army's probable concentration point. Stuart prepared directives for his brigades based on this third communique and issued them the next day. Leaving two brigades behind, Jeb believed he had left 9,000 troopers available to Robert E. Lee. On June 25 at 1:00 am, Stuart led the remaining three brigades—over 4,000 strong—east over the Bull Run mountains and into the rear of the Army of The Potomac.

As the column snaked towards Haymarket, the Yankees seemed everywhere. Stuart had hoped to swing north before reaching Centreville, but the enemy presence there forced him to improvise. The next day, the column veered southeast through Brentsville before halting at Wolf Run Shoals on the Occoquan. Around this time, Jeb committed to crossing the Potomac east of the Blue Ridge. Accordingly, on the morning of the 27th, Stuart ordered Fitz Lee to Burke's Station while the main force swept towards Fairfax Court House. During the ride, Stuart had scouted well ahead of the troopers, barely avoiding capture by an enemy mounted party. Then came word from Fitz Lee that the route to Rowser's Ford on the Potomac was open. Around sundown, Hampton arrived only to find the ford two feet higher than its normal depth. But Stuart had been in this predicament before: through the night the horsemen simply hauled their equipment submerged through the waist-deep water. Sometime before dawn on June 28, the three brigades had crossed safely into Maryland.

Jeb was now fully committed to encircling the Yankee army and combining with Jubal Early who had coincidently arrived in York, Pennsylvania this same day. Stuart, however, still had some 60 miles to go. After cutting the C&O Canal and capturing a number of supply boats, the rebels rode north to Rockville, arriving there about noon. Athwart the Federal supply line, Confederate scouts soon reported the approach of a massive enemy wagon train from the southeast, and in no time, Stuart's boys captured 125 wagons brimming with supplies. Loaded with the booty, the General actually contemplated carrying the raid into

Washington. Instead he pushed north to Brookeville, reaching town that night. There he paroled some 400 of his prisoners before moving on to Cooksville, where he paroled the rest. At dawn, June 29, his main body dismantled the Baltimore & Ohio Railroad at Sykesville and Hood's Mill, while an advance party cleared Westminster. Stuart brought the column together to camp that evening at Union Mills.

On June 30, the cavalry crossed into Pennsylvania. Chambliss led the column towards Hanover where, about mid-day, he detected a large detachment of enemy horse, which Stuart vigorously attacked. During the fight Hampton began working his way around the enemy's left flank and gained the road to York. Realizing that little was being accomplished, Stuart disengaged his troops and moved towards York via Jefferson. By now, the men were exhausted, and even Stuart was aware the wagon train had become a "serious embarrassment." But Lee's orders called for the collection of supplies, and Jeb was committed to bringing the prizes in. Years later, William Blackford bemoaned the movement away from Gettysburg: "If we could have made our way direct, the fifteen miles of distance...would have passed that day."

After a soul-sapping night march, the column halted for a brief rest near Dover. Here Stuart made a startling discovery. Some days earlier, Jubal Early had passed through town headed for York but had since doubled back towards Gettysburg. Stuart sent two staff officers to find Early while ordering his men northwest to Dillsburg. Toward night, the bedraggled column reached Carlisle, where they found a large Union cavalry garrison in residence. With rumors flying that a local militia group lay in ambush, Stuart's horse artillery unlimbered and threw a few shells into the town, igniting some buildings in the Carlisle Barracks. Beyond exhaustion, many of the gunners were falling asleep at their pieces. Just then, a courier galloped up, bringing word of the day's engagement at Gettysburg and Lee's orders for Stuart to lead his troopers there at once. Leaving Fitz Lee in Carlisle, Jeb ordered the column in motion and with a small group of staff officers rode south in advance.

After a two hour nap in mid-ride, Stuart left his slumbering coterie and proceeded to Lee's headquarters, arriving sometime near mid-day of July 2. Lee's reaction to Stuart's arrival has been variously described as "Well, General Stuart, you are here at last," and "General Stuart, where have you been?" Even officers who weren't present had their own version of events: Henry McClellan claimed it was "painful beyond description" though he was miles away at the time. In his battle report,

Lee would say "The movements of the army preceding the battle of Gettysburg had been much embarrassed by the absence of the cavalry," while exonerating Stuart of any wrongdoing: "In the exercise of the discretion given him when Longstreet and Hill marched into Maryland, General Stuart determined to pass around the rear of the Federal Army." Nonetheless, Stuart was stung by Lee's words, and he specificly addressed them in his own report of the campaign: "The cavalry specially selected for advance guard...by the commanding general...(Jenkin's brigade, left in the rear) was not as efficient as it ought to have been." However, Stuart staffer Henry McClellan summed it up best:"It was not want of cavalry that General Lee bewailed...It was the absence of Stuart himself."

GETTYSBURG

Arriving at Gettysburg, Stuart's troopers went into camp and attempted to recoup from their ordeal. Towards late afternoon, however, Hampton's brigade was forced to fend off a determined enemy thrust northeast of Gettysburg near Hunterstown, and elements of Cobb's Legion suffered in the melee. As darkness came on, the battle turned into an artillery duel which ended in a draw. Afterwards, most of Hampton's troopers simply collapsed along their line. Meanwhile a weary Jeb Stuart worked doggedly to secure the army's left flank. Finally, he and his men were able to camp and get their first good sleep in a week.

The following day—July 3—in accordance with Lee's orders to protect the Confederate left, Stuart led some 5,000 men and fourteen guns two and a half miles east on the York Turnpike. The column then angled down a narrow farm lane, the lead brigades forming a line behind a forested ridge to await Hampton and Fitz Lee's troopers. Mysteriously, Stuart then ordered a gun from Captain Thomas Jackson's battery to fire a shot in each direction of the compass, an action he chose never to explain. Near noon, enemy artillery one mile south near the Hanover Road replied, thus beginning Jeb Stuart's own battle of Gettysburg.

The General claimed later that he had kept the lead brigades— Witcher and Chambliss' men—hidden in an effort to surprise the Yankee cavalry visible along the Hanover Road. However, as Hampton and Lee's brigades arrived, the horsemen crossed the high ground—known locally as Cress Ridge—and advanced south onto the open farmland. Union horse immediately maneuvered to counter their appearance. His hopes for surprise now frustrated, Stuart posted Witcher with a strong

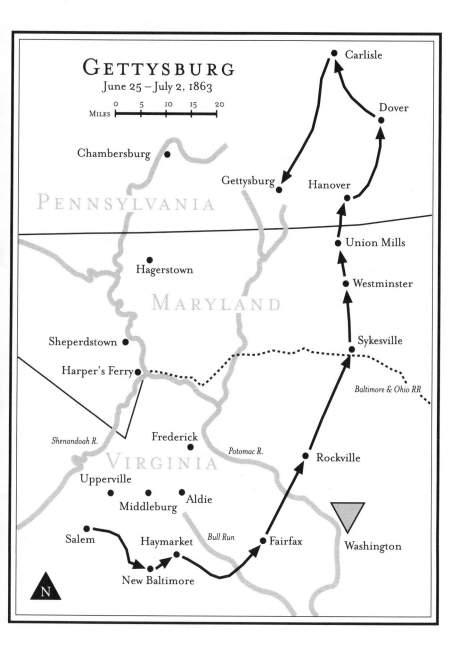

GETTYSBURG
June 25 – July 2, 1863

MILES 0 5 10 15 20

Carlisle

Dover

Chambersburg

Gettysburg   Hanover

PENNSYLVANIA

Union Mills

Hagerstown   Westminster

MARYLAND

Sheperdstown   Sykesville

Harper's Ferry   Baltimore & Ohio RR

Shenandoah R.   Frederick   Potomac R.   Rockville

VIRGINIA

Upperville

Middleburg   Aldie

Salem   Bull Run   Fairfax

Haymarket   Washington

New Baltimore

N

skirmish line along a fenceline south of the Rummel Farm parallel to the enemy advance and ordered him to engage the Yankees. He planned to use this force to mask Hampton and Lee's movement by the rear against the enemy left: "I sent for them to come forward...and arrange further operations." Meanwhile, Witcher's men slugged it out on their line for a full two hours until Fitz Lee advanced his own skirmishers against the Northerners' right flank. The enemy withdrew east to a woodlot, but as the Confederates fanned out in pursuit, a dismounted Federal regiment armed with Spencer repeating rifles charged up from the south and drove Witcher's men past their original position. Stuart sensed an opportunity and ordered Chambliss to crush the Federal right with a mounted charge. As elements of the 9th and 13th Virginia burst from the Cress woods, the reeling Yankees gamely refused their right flank, but the Southern pressure soon forced the enemy—Spencers and all—to the south.

Federal artillery now began roaring from positions along the Hanover Road. Suddenly, a full regiment of Yankee cavalry—the 7th Michigan led by newly-minted Brigadier General George Custer—swept the Confederates back "from field to field" to a position along two fence lines. The Michiganders charged right up... "literally face to face with the foe," until the troopers of the1st Virginia arrived to bolster their comrades. Stuart then committed two of Hampton's regiments to the fray, directing the troopers to swing around their compatriots and strike the Federal left. Custer saw the danger and pulled his men south, but the 1st Virginia—Stuart's old command—pushed on in a charge "not only extraordinary, but irresistible," galloping nearly to the muzzles of the Federal artillery. But, weakened horseflesh, stinging flank fire, and the roiling presence of enemy reinforcements finally forced the Virginians back.

For a second time, mounted Federals galloped north in the wake of the Confederate retreat. The Confederates reacted in kind. Wade Hampton had come forward with the remainder of his brigade to rally his 1st North Carolina and the Jeff Davis Legion, while Fitz Lee committed his brigade in an assault Stuart had not wanted ("I would have perferred a different method of attack.") Nonetheless, the 1,500 Southerners advanced "as if on review, with sabers drawn and glistening like silver," eliciting murmurs of admiration from their foe. Unfortunately, the sturdy fencelines funnelled the charge into hellacious fire, with dismounted Yankees punishing the flanks with carbine fire. Federal cavalry then slammed violently into the head of the column, while smaller units struck at the flanks. In the melee, Wade Hampton went down with a saber wound to the head, and Fitz Lee fought a desperate hand to hand duel for his life.

Finally, after ten minutes of jarring confrontation, it was over. The Confederates reluctantly fell back past the Rummel farm as Stuart deployed Witcher's men to discourage pursuit, while the Northerners fell back towards the Hanover Road.

Following the Federal repulse of Pickett's Charge, Robert E. Lee decided to withdraw his battered army south of the Potomac. "Marse Robert" called upon Stuart and his troopers to defend the flanks of the retreating columns, and for the next 10 days the Confederate horse held off determined thrusts by the Federal cavalry. On the 6th, as John Buford poked at the Confederate wagon park near Williamsport, Stuart concentrated much of his command at Hagerstown and punished a Yankee force advancing from Boonsboro. He then covered the arrival of Lee's army, fending off powerful Federal forays on the 10th and the 12th. However, the combined strain of fatigue and high command was beginning to tell as the General seemed to sleepwalk rudely through a Hagerstown dinner. Despite the sleepless nights and the reverses of the previous month, Stuart's own spirits remained high: "General Lee's manuevering the Yankees out of Virginia is the grandest piece of strategy ever heard of (and) My Cavalry is the finest body of men 'on the planet.'" Concerning his part in the campaign, Jeb simply stated, "I had a grand time in Pennsylvania and we return without defeat."

AUTUMN

On July 14, Stuart covered Lee's retreat across the Potomac and into Virginia. Eventually the opposing armies fell into a standoff along the Rappahannock River, where Robert E. Lee announced the reorganization of the Confederate cavalry. Stuart was to command two 3-brigade divisions—Wade Hampton's and Fitzhugh Lee's—but would not receive a promotion to Lieutenant General as he had hoped. Despite the banishment of Beverly Robertson to South Carolina, Stuart failed to secure promotion for two of his favorites, Tom Munford and Tom Rosser. In bitterness, Rosser privately accused his commander of infidelity, marital and otherwise. But the war intervened to put an end to personal squabbles. On September 13, the Federals forced the Rappahannock and pushed Stuart back to the Rapidan. However, when Union cavalry attempted to flank Lee's left, Stuart and his troopers blunted the effort. Forced to fight in two directions, Stuart managed to frustrate both John Buford and Judson Kilpatrick's divisions near Jack's Shop. When the

Federal horse withdrew to the north, it was then "Marse Robert's" turn to seize the initiative.

Determined to attack Meade's right to the north of the Rappahannock, Lee sent Stuart forth to screen the advance. On October 11, his cavalry flanked Kilpatrick near Culpeper and rode hard for Fleetwood Heights north of Brandy Station. Unfortunately, Kilpatrick and Buford won the race for the high ground and managed to fend Stuart off. On the 13th, Jeb brought three brigades near Catlett's Station, where he found the rear of Meade's army marching north along the railroad. Suddenly disaster loomed as Stuart's own scouts discovered another large Federal column was moving on a parallel road to the west. To all appearances, Stuart seemed trapped.

Rising to the occasion, Jeb drew his men into a small valley near the hamlet of Auburn and hid them so well that they literally disappeared. With Yankees bedding down not more than 150 yards away, Confederate troopers spent a tense, hushed night. However, soon after daylight, sounds of battle echoed up from the west. Stuart's pleas for help had brought Richard Ewell's infantry slamming into the Federal rear, which enabled Jeb to advanced his artillery and bring his troopers charging out of the woods. Ever resourceful, Stuart had evaded another snare.

In the end, Lee's attempts to bag George Meade came to naught. When the latter assumed a strong defensive stance near the old Manassas battlefields, Lee withdrew back across the Rappahannock. While screening this retrograde movement, Stuart's men were aggressively set upon by Kilpatrick's bluecoats near the town of Buckland. On October 19, in conjunction with Fitz Lee, Stuart craftily drew the Yankees further south, then turned to attack their head while Lee crushed their rear. The resultant rout—the so-called "Buckland Races"— provided one of the most embarrassing moments in the history of Yankee cavalry. However, Buckland was but a footnote to a month of inconclusive manuevering. By November 9, the two armies were settled in a face-off along the Rapidan.

In late November, Meade made one more attempt to come to grips with Lee, this time near a stream called Mine Run. Stuart performed what little cavalry work was required and spent most of his time commanding Wade Hampton's division. However, the Federal movement ground down, and, giving it up, Meade had returned to camp north of the Rappahannock as the sides settled into winter quarters.

1864

Daunting difficulties faced the cavalry of the Army of Northern Virginia in the early months of 1864, as the corrosion of war wasted southern horseflesh. Moreover, despite their humiliation in the "Buckland Races," the Union cavalry had become a formidable opponent. Everywhere, it seemed, the fortunes of the Confederacy were ebbing, and rebel spirits flagged in consequence. But Jeb Stuart remained true to the cause and made the rounds from Fredricksburg to Richmond acting the role of the Bold Cavalier. He all but ordered Flora to cease wearing mourning clothes for their deceased, and, he christened his new daughter Virgina Pelham in honor of his home state and the fallen artillerist. At a series of balls, Stuart stoked the Southern spirit, appearing to all as "the gayest of the gay." In Richmond, he took part in an elaborate game of charades where, to the strains of "See! The Conquering Hero Comes," he offered his sword on the altar of the Confederacy. Perhaps some were losing heart, but Jeb Stuart would be ever true to the Southern Cause.

Only once did the war disturb the winter interlude. On February 28, Custer and his troopers burst past the Confederate left and rode hard for Charlottesville while Judson Kilpatrick descended on Richmond. In miserable weather, Stuart pounded in pursuit of Custer with a fraction of Wickham's command. Stuart's troopers, however, felt a different kind of sting when Custer merely brushed them aside on his return from the raid. Highly disappointed in his troopers, Jeb then drove his men east but arrived too late to bag Kilpatrick. "It was evident that he (Stuart) didn't think well of the past two days' proceedings," wrote staffmember Theodore Garnett. In all, it was another frustrating effort for the increasingly bedraggled Southern cavalry.

Towards the end of April, Stuart's scouts confirmed the inevitable: the Army of the Potomac and its new commander-in-chief General Ulysses S. Grant were preparing to march south. On May 4, with the Yankees streaming over the Rapidan fords, Stuart pressed east on the Orange-Fredricksburg Plank Road into the haunts of the Wilderness. Somewhere in the vine-choked woods, Jeb encountered the Federals. Illuminated by the setting sun, the cavalryman retraced his tracks and found A.P. Hill's advancing infantry and Hampton's horsemen. With bonfires lighting the roadways, the men of both service arms made the forest tremble with their ringing salutes to the cavalry commander, "his plumed hat in hand...both man and horse being as motionless as marble."

The next morning, May 5, Jeb led Hill's advance to the point of the previous day's contact. As the opponents stumbled into each other's path, the battle of the Wilderness ignited in bloody confusion. Stuart as usual was everywhere, but at the end of the two days of inconclusive fighting, was able to write Flora that "I am safe and well tonight." When Ulysses Grant moved south by Lee's right flank, Stuart guided the Army of Northern Virginia southeast into position while Fitz Lee fought a desperate action near Spotsylvania Court House. On May 8, with Stuart commanding both cavalry and infantry, the Confederates won the race to the strategic crossroads, and the two sides were soon slugging it out west and north of the town.

TWILIGHT

When Grant assumed supreme Federal command, he installed the Irish firebrand Phil Sheridan as cavalry chief of the Army of the Potomac. Sheridan quickly showed his spirit, angrily demanding that he be let loose to "thrash hell out of (Stuart)." Grant gave Sheridan carte blanche to do just that, and, on May 9, "Little Phil" trotted east from Spotsylvania then south on the Telegraph Road towards Richmond, looking for Stuart and some Confederate cavalry to thrash. Apprised of the development, Jeb gathered three brigades totalling some 4500 troopers and took up the gauntlet.

The gray troopers rode all day and into the night, arriving at a plundered Beaver Dam Station during the early morning of the 10th. As his horsemen paused, Stuart and Reid Venable rode to the home of Edmund Fontaine where Flora and the children had taken refuge. The couple spoke briefly, whereupon the cavalryman bent from his horse and kissed his Flora goodby. In departing, Jeb bleakly muttered that he didn't believe he would survive the war and didn't care to if the Confederacy lost.

Stuart now divided the Confederate column, sending one brigade under General James Gordon to track the enemy rear, while the other two brigades circled the enemy's route to gain their front. Jeb rode with Fitz Lee in the latter column, and, sometime after midnight on Lee's insistance, they bivuoacked near Hanover Junction. Some three hours later, they were again on the move, winding down the Telegraph Road with a "softer, more communicative" Stuart in the lead. Around mid-morning they reached an intersection called Yellow Tavern, just six miles from the Richmond defenses. Presuming that the capital's defenses could withstand an enemy thrust, Jeb aligned his 1,100 men in a dismounted battleline facing west with his left anchored on the Tavern. Scouts had located Sheridan's column north and west of Stuart on the Mountain Road, a track that intersected the Telegraph Road near the Tavern. As the sun heated the morning air, the rumble of Gordon's encounter with the Federal rear echoed far to the north. Finally, around noon, the Yankees arrived.

The first enemy foray circled Stuart's flank near the Tavern, forcing his leftmost units northward. As the Confederates struggled to realign, the Federals launched another attack. As the two lines came to desperate grips, Jeb charged from point to threatened point, encouraging his men to hold their ground. Warned that he was dangerously exposing himself, the General chuckled and said, "I don't reckon there is any danger." However, as more and more dismounted Bluecoats swept out of the woodlots, a mounted column thundered up and scythed Stuart's sagging line. The fight was close, but the battered Confederates held on and reformed facing to the south across the Telegraph Road. Jeb now sent word to Richmond that he could hold his position if only the Home Guard would be marched out to catch Sheridan in a pincer. Eventually the Unionist wave receeded, and, as the opposing sides paused to perfect their alignments, a lull descended on the field.

Around 4:00 p.m., the Federals came on again, this time in overwhelming numbers. Stuart rode towards his left where the threat appeared gravest. Arriving at a point where the Telegraph Road intersected his battleline, Jeb reined his horse up to a fenceline along the west side of the road and sandwiched himself between two members of the 1st Virginia, his old regiment. As the enemy swept past their position, the General bellowed, "Boys, don't stop to count fours. Shoot them! Shoot them!" Ever setting the example, Jeb levelled his pistol and blasted away. One Virginian heard him roar,"Steady, men, steady!" Blue clad horsemen, mounted and dismounted, fought their way past the Confederate line, prompting Stuart to call out, "Bully for Old K! Give it to 'em boys!" Chaos reigned.

A Confederate countercharge sealed the breakthrough and pushed the enemy horsemen south, with Jeb and his boys pricking at their flanks. Out in the roadway, one of the sprinting Federals, a dismounted Michigander turned his pistol toward the oncoming Confederates and fired. The bullet flashed across the short interval and tore into the Stuart's right side, just under his ribcage. With some difficulty, his men lifted him from his horse and placed him in an ambulance directed to the rear. By this time, however, more Federal brigades had entered the assault, and, as the Confederate retreat became a rout, the ambulance was nearly taken. Somehow, the driver managed to guide the wagon to safety.

It was well into the evening before Stuart's ambulance could complete its circuitous route into Richmond. Once within the city, Jeb was gingerly carried into the house of his brother-in-law where an attending physicians declared him mortally wounded. As word spread of his presence there, a crowd gathered to keep vigil. Throughout the night and into the next day, a procession of Confederate officers and dignitaries wound through the house paying their last respects, holding final, hushed conversations with the dying cavalryman. Towards the evening, the death pall began to cast its inevitable shadow. Those keeping watch joined in a hymn while Jeb made his peace with his God. "I am going fast now," he was heard to mumble, then admitted, "I am resigned; God's will be done." Finally, near 8:00 pm, as the sun set on the war-ravaged city, Major General James Ewell Brown Stuart breathed his last.

Flora arrived sometime before midnight. The General's pockets had been emptied, and the widow found a letter discussing Jeb's plans to bring her to headquarters once Sheridan's raid was supressed. She also discovered his congratulatory order to the infantrymen he commanded at Chancellorsville. Even in her grief, the last two items found must have spurred deep emotions: a poem about the death of a child and a lock of Little Flora's hair. She would wear widow's black until the day she died, May 10, 1923.

On May 13, with the roar of battle echoing from the front, Jeb Stuart was laid to rest in Richmond's Hollywood Cemetery. Out in the Shenandoah Valley, a stunned Grumble Jones exclaimed, "(This) is the greatest loss the army has ever sustained except the death of Jackson." Up near Spotsylvania, Robert E. Lee stoically reflected upon his cavalry commander and remarked, "He never brought me a piece of false information." But later, when the full import of his loss became apparent, Lee revealed, "I can scarcely think of him without weeping."

Author Note: Patrick Brennan is a native of Chicago, Illinois, and a life long student of the American Civil War. A rock, blues, and country keyboard player by trade, he is the author of *Secessionville: Assault on Charleston.*

AFTERWORD

Some men are born to write great works, others to paint great pictures, others to rule over nations. Stuart was born to fight cavalry.

—John Esten Cooke

As the great grandson of General J.E.B. Stuart, I have often been asked for an opinion of this great man's legacy to the nation, and how he should be remembered. Although my answer has changed, as I have grown older, one central theme has endured through time. He was a man who fought for a cause that he deeply believed in with a tenacity and a steadfast commitment that is remarkable by any standard. Two excerpts from a letter that he wrote his wife Flora in 1862 speaks volumes in explaining this dedication and commitment: "I, for one, though I stood alone in the Confederacy, without countenance or aid, would uphold the banner of Southern Independence as long as I had a hand left to grasp the staff, and then die before submitting..." "Tell my boy when I am gone how I felt and wrote and tell him...never to forget the principles for which his father struggled."

Another element of the Stuart legacy became evident to me only after I had served a good portion of a twenty seven year career in the United States Army. It was not until then that I began to realize and appreciate his accomplishments as a professional soldier—accomplishments made possible by four personal characteristics which seem to me as essential to success in military life today as they were in Jeb Stuart's time.

First of all, Stuart knew how to organize and lead men in combat; his situational assessment skills were truly second to none; he had no equal in technical proficiency in the deployment and use of cavalry, and he continally demonstrated that he was capable of leading larger units with expanded missions and responsibilities. This last characteristic is the distinguishing hallmark of soldiers destined for high command.

Along with these essential personal characteristics, Stuart possessed the true "Warrior Spirit", combined a love of horses and horsemanship. As a young West Point cadet he wrote to a friend: "...so far I know no other profession more desirable than that of a soldier, indeed, everything connected with the military has far surpassed my most sanguine expectations." Horse soldiering was to be his vocation—his trade, craft, and art rolled into one.

Before the American Civil War Stuart's military skills were sharply honed during seven years as a lieutenant on the western frontier, most of it in cavalry service. On the frontier his professional proficiency was acknowledged by many, including Major John Sedgwick who served with him from 1855 to 1860 in the U.S. 1st Cavalry Regiment. Later on, as a Union general, Sedgewick would pay Stuart the supreme compliment, referring to him as "the finest Cavalry Officer ever foaled in America."

During the Civil War Stuart received rapid promotion, passing from Lieutenant Colonel to Brigadier General at age 28; to Major General at age 29, the rank he held when mortally wounded at 31. More important than his rise in rank was the role he played in the evolution of cavalry doctrine. Readers should understand that General Stuart came on the scene when the mission of cavalry was in a difficult transitional phase. The U.S. Army Cavalry manual of the time—written by General Philip St. George Cooke, Stuart's father-in-law—spoke of the "Charge" as being the most decisive element in cavalry tactics. Was this really the case, or was cavalry moving in a different direction prompted by development of the cone shaped bullet, the rifling concept and rapid fire weapons? I think the latter.

General Stuart quickly became an agent for change. Confederate forces under his guidance established early a centralized command for cavalry operations which stressed five basic functions: (1) Reconnaissance (2) Counter Reconnaissance or Denial Operations (3) Screening (4) Security (5) Reconnaissance in Force. These new functions represented revolutionary change in cavalry operational concepts. I contend that if you were to visit an Armored Cavalry Regiment today and ask the Commanding Officer to describe the unit's mission he would describe it in terms very similar to those which evolved during the Civil War.

To my mind, General Stuart played a major role in developing the doctrines that have shaped the mobile warfare of today. I believe that this contribution deserves wider recognition than it has received, and is the often overlooked legacy of this great American soldier.

Colonel J.E.B. Stuart IV, U.S.A. (Ret.)
Richmond, VA

Reader's Note: The footnotes and the complete bibliography this work have been place on file for viewing purposes at the Gettysburg National Military Park library. Readers may obtain a set of footnotes and the complete bibliography by sending $2.00 to the Farnsworth House Book Shop, 415 Baltimore Street, Gettysburg, PA 17325.

SELECT BIBLIOGRAPHY

Blackford, Charles. *War Years With Jeb Stuart*. New York: Scribner's Sons. 1945.

Cooke, John Esten. *Wearing Of The Gray*. Bloomington: Indiana University Press. 1959.

Davis, Burke. *Jeb Stuart, The Last Cavalier*. New York: Holt, Rinehart and Winston, Inc. 1957.

Eggleston, George Cary. *A Rebel's Recollection*. Bloomington: Indiana University Press. 1959.

McClellan, H.B. *I Rode With Jeb Stuart*. Bloomington: Indiana University Press. 1958.

Mitchell, Adele H. (ed.). *The Letters Of General JEB Stuart*. Stuart-Mosby Historical Society. 1990.

Nesbitt, Mark. *Saber and Scapegoat*. Mechanicsburg: Stackpole Books. 1994.

Thomas, Emory. *Bold Dragoon*. New York: Harper & Row. 1986.

Thomason, John W. *Jeb Stuart*. New York: Scribner's Sons. 1929.

Trout, Robert. *They Followed The Plume*. Mechanicsburg: Stackpole Books. 1993.

Trout, Robert. *With Pen & Saber*. Mechanicsburg: Stackpole Books. 1995.

Von Borke, Heros. *Memoirs Of The Confederate War*. Dayton: Morningside. 1985.

FARNSWORTH HOUSE PUBLICATIONS

"TRUST IN GOD AND FEAR NOTHING" GENERAL LEWIS A. ARMISTEAD, CSA, by Wayne E. Motts, w/afterword by Lewis B. Armistead. Farnsworth House Civil War Commander Series #1.

"THE DEVIL'S TO PAY" GENERAL JOHN BUFORD, USA, by Michael Phipps and John Peterson, w/afterword by Senator Tom Buford. Farnsworth House Commander Series #2.

"FAITHFULLY AND FOREVER YOUR SOLDIER" GENERAL GEORGE E. PICKETT, CSA, by Richard F. Selcer, w/afterword by George E. Pickett. Farnsworth House Commander Series #3.

"FOR GOD'S SAKE FORWARD" GENERAL JOHN F. REYNOLDS, USA, by Michael A. Riley, afterword by Alan T. Nolan. Farnsworth House Commander Series #4.

"COME ON YOU WOLVERINES!" CUSTER AT GETTYSBURG, by Michael Phipps, w/afterword by Paul Andrew Hutton. Commander Series #5.

"DUTY FAITHFULLY PERFORMED" GENERAL ROBERT E. LEE, CSA, by Gary W. Gallagher. Farnsworth House Commander Series #6.

"...LIKE A STONE WALL" GENERAL THOMAS J. JACKSON by Robert K. Krick. Commander Series #7.

"I WILL HAVE JUSTICE DONE" GENERAL GOUVERNEUR K. WARREN by Michael T. Kelly. Farnsworth House Commander Series #8.

"I HAVE BEEN A SOLDIER ALL MY LIFE" GEN. JAMES LONGSTREET, CSA by Carol Reardon. Farnsworth House Commander Series #9.

TRAVELLER & COMPANY: THE HORSES OF GETTYSBURG, by Blake A. Magner, w/foreword by Mark Meyers.

THE BATTLE OF GETTYSBURG, by Major General George Gordon Meade. (Self contained extract from General Meade's Life and Letters, edited by his son).

KELLY'S HEROES: THE IRISH BRIGADE AT GETTYSBURG, by T. L. Murphy.